POSSESSING
THE MIND OF CHRIST

by Frances Hunter

Published by
HUNTER I
City of I
201 McClell
Kingwood, Texa:

BOOKS BY CHARLES ❤ FRANCES HUNTER

A CONFESSION A DAY KEEPS THE DEVIL AWAY
ANGELS ON ASSIGNMENT
ARE YOU TIRED?
BORN AGAIN! WHAT DO YOU MEAN?
COME ALIVE
DELIGHTFULLY CHARISMATIC Christian Walk Seminar Manual
DEVIL, YOU CAN'T STEAL WHAT'S MINE
DON'T LIMIT GOD
DON'T PANIC...PRAY!
FOLLOW ME
GOD IS FABULOUS
GOD'S ANSWER TO FAT...LOØSE IT!
GOD'S BIG "IF"
GOD'S CONDITIONS FOR PROSPERITY
HOT LINE TO HEAVEN
HOW TO DEVELOP YOUR FAITH
HOW TO FIND GOD'S WILL FOR YOUR LIFE
HOW TO HAVE FREEDOM FROM FEAR
HOW TO MAKE YOUR MARRIAGE EXCITING
IMPOSSIBLE MIRACLES
IN JESUS' NAME!
INVEST YOUR LIFE IN GOD
IT'S SO SIMPLE (formerly HANG LOOSE WITH JESUS)
JOY, JOY, JOY!
LET'S GO WITNESSING (formerly GO, MAN, GO)
MEMORIZING MADE EASY
MY LOVE AFFAIR WITH CHARLES
NUGGETS OF TRUTH
POSSESSING THE MIND OF CHRIST
P.T.L.A. (Praise the Lord, Anyway!)
SIMPLE AS A.B.C.
SINCE JESUS PASSED BY
SHOUT THE WORD
the fabulous SKINNIE MINNIE RECIPE BOOK
SUPERNATURAL HORIZONS (from Glory to Glory)
THE DEVIL WANTS YOUR MIND
THE TWO SIDES OF A COIN
THIS WAY UP!
TO HEAL THE SICK
WHY SHOULD "I" SPEAK IN TONGUES???

Scripture quotations are taken from:
The New King James Version, used throughout unless otherwise stated.
© 1983 by Thomas Nelson, Inc., Nashville, Tennessee.
The Authorized King James Version (KJV)
The Living Bible, Paraphrased (TLB),
© 1971 by Tyndale House Publishers, Wheaton, Illinois.
The Amplified Old Testament (Amp.),
© 1965 by Zondervan Publishing.
The Amplified New Testament (Amp.),
© The Lockman Foundation 1954, 1958.
ISBN 0-917726-64-2

TABLE OF CONTENTS

WHAT DOES JESUS SAY ABOUT:

Sacrifice of Praise

Deliverance, Trust
[Fear, Afraid]

For information about the City of Light Video teaching tapes, audio tapes, price list of Hunter Books, write to:

HUNTER BOOKS
City of Light
201 McClellan Road
Kingwood, Texas 77339, U.S.A

In the event your Christian Bookstore does not have any of the books written by Charles and Frances Hunter or published by Hunter Books, please write for price list and order form from HUNTER BOOKS.

CHAPTER ONE

WHAT DOES JESUS SAY ABOUT "THINKING HIS THOUGHTS"

The magnitude of God's love for us and what He does for us at the very moment of our spiritual conception when we are born again by the Spirit of God is one of the most awe-inspiring miracles in the world.

When we sincerely receive the revelation of what we actually acquire as a born-again child of God, it takes us into a supernatural realm that is so far beyond our human ability to understand that we should all fall on our faces and worship God the Father.

To me, one of the most exciting realms into which God takes us is in I Corinthians 2:16 concerning the fact that we actually possess the mind of Christ. I especially love the way it is expressed in the

Praise the Lord "
Spirt of the living I will TRUST in You

Amplified Bible, *"But we have the mind of Christ, the Messiah, and do hold the thoughts (feelings and purposes) of His heart."*

God loves us so much that He is willing to take our dirty, sinful minds (remember those dirty jokes you used to tell and dirty thoughts you used to think?) and replace them with the actual mind of Christ so that we have His thoughts, His feelings, His attitudes, and His purposes instilled and placed into what was formerly our old nature. What kind of a God is this that He can love us that much?

Philippians 2:5 says, *"Let this mind be in you which was also in Christ Jesus."* The very thought that God would let the mind of Christ be in us is so supernatural that it is impossible for the natural mind to understand; however, the thing that is so totally and completely exciting about this is what happens to our lives as we begin to realize and accept the fact that we DO have the mind of Christ.

How should we think?

How should we act?

How should we behave?

How should we know the answers to all these questions? It is so easy if we just understand the principles of possessing the mind of Christ.

All the way throughout his lifetime, Paul taught about the mystery of the ages, which was, *"Christ in you, the hope of Glory"* (Colossians 1:27). Many people cannot grasp the promise that when we are born again by the Spirit of God, Jesus Christ comes to live His life *in* and *through* us. We actually have the Spirit of Christ, His ability, and His power locked up within us when we are born again by the Spirit of God.

When I think that we have the actual mind of Christ, it is difficult for me to even stay on this earth. I feel like I could go into orbit and never come back again when I realize that God has placed in our hands such a priceless possession as the very mind of Christ.

The questions asked us more than any other are, "How do I know the will of God?" "What am I supposed to do as a Christian?" "How am I supposed to act?"

It is so easy to find out! All you have to do is open the Bible!

Pick up a red-letter edition of the Bible. Each time you see the red letters, you know that is what Jesus said. If we say and believe the words that Jesus says and then act upon them, we will be operating with the mind of Christ.

Many people have a possession, but never enjoy it, never use it, and never get anything out of it. This is what happens to many people concerning the invaluable possession of the actual mind of Christ.

We may have the priceless opportunity to possess it, but we can never really possess it until we are willing to totally and completely submerge our own personality, will, and intellect into the mind of Christ and let Him begin to operate in and through us. The day that the Body of Christ learns to do this is going to be the day when the wraps will be taken off of the power of God! The devil will KNOW he has to run, and the Body of Christ will finally fully understand that the devil HAS TO RUN. Because we possess the very mind of Christ we have all power in heaven and in earth!

Any of the gospels in the New Testament will start you on the road to discovering how to react under ALL circumstances, simply because we possess the mind of Christ!

In Luke 4:4 it says, *"It is written, man shall not live by bread alone, but by every word of God."*

If we are going to operate with the mind of Christ, if we are going to literally possess the mind of Christ, then we are going to have to believe what this says. We are not going to live by physical food alone, but we are going to live by spiritual food which is the Word of God. If we are going to LIVE by every Word of God, then we certainly need to know what the Word of God says. Only then can we sit ourselves down to a beautiful and exciting feast all of the time. He places His Spirit in us when we receive the gift of the Holy Spirit. Therein lies our source of power to give life to the Word.

The Word of God, or the Word that God speaks, is alive and full of power making it active, operative, energizing, and effective. Do you realize that if we live by the Word of God, we will be full of power? We will be operative! We will be energized. We will be able to be alive in Christ and effective at all times. There is no physical food that will give you the same type of energy, power, wisdom, and discernment as the Word of God.

Why is the Word of God so powerful? Because our all-powerful God is the one who spoke the Word and He personally backs what He says.

There have been many times when I have been so exhausted I felt I could not go on — times when my body has cried out for sleep and rest. Instead, I have gone into the Word of God and come out of the pages an actual tiger with no lack of energy! NOTHING will inject energy and power into your mind and body like God's Word! So, if we are going to live and breathe and be energized and empowered by every Word of God, then we certainly need to know what the Word of God says.

Let us go to the 8th verse in that same chapter. It says, *"And Jesus answered and said unto him, Get thee behind me, Satan; for it is written, Thou shalt worship the Lord thy God, and him only shalt thou serve"*(KJV). If we have the mind of Christ, what are we going to be doing? We are going to worship the Lord. We will not worship anything else.

We are not going to worship TV!

We are not going to worship movies!

We are not going to worship homes!

We are not going to worship fancy clothes!

We are not going to worship undesirable habits and attitudes which actually is worshipping only ourselves.

We are going to worship the Lord.

There are many people who worship a television set. They will sit in front of it and worship it for hours. They will sit and watch soap operas hour after hour knowing full well that there is nothing spiritual, nothing to be gained, nothing that will uplift them and nothing that will edify them as they watch the humdrum TV programs day after day.

If we are going to truly operate with the mind of Christ, then we are going to do exactly what Jesus did. We are going to worship the Lord and nothing else! All of these things become obsolete when we really put Jesus first in our life. Suddenly, the things of this world will grow strangely dim in the light of His glory and grace if we really keep our eyes on Jesus. Therefore, because we have the mind of Christ, we are not going to worship the things of the world.

We are not going to worship golf games on Sunday instead of going to church.

We are not going to worship fishing and boats; we are not going to worship guns or trophies!

We are not going to worship vacations over serving God!

We are not going to worship entertainment, country clubs or other worldly things over the things of God. *"Do not love the world or the things in the world. If anyone loves the world, the love of the Father is not in him"* (I John 2:15).

When we really let the mind of Christ actually possess us, and when we possess the mind of Christ, our mind will be thinking in exactly the same directions as Jesus does. Our answers will be the same as His, and our dedicated, daily life will be the same as His. We will be out there doing exactly the same things Jesus did!

Here is something that is going to "get" a lot of people. That's why I decided to put this in at the very beginning of the the book. One of the most difficult areas for many individuals to use the attitude of Christ is in the area of finances. We don't have difficulty wanting to believe to receive from God, but we have problems in giving to God.

This area is so important in my life because God dealt with me within seconds after I had been born again. I had not even been saved a split-second when the almighty God spoke to me. His words changed my entire thinking about giving.

I had always been a real tight-wad where giving to God was concerned. I never went to church without checking first to see that I had a single one dollar bill in my wallet. There wasn't a preacher in the world who was going to "get" more than a dollar out of me. It would have never entered my mind to give a five dollar bill, a ten or twenty. Twenty dollars would have meant that I was a spendthrift!

God always knows exactly how to deal with us on the level where we are. I had not even been saved more than two seconds when God spoke to me.

There was no doubt in my mind it was God. I had gone from sinner to saint and in less than two seconds God was already speaking to me! I was overjoyed!

The God who made the universe had taken time out to speak to me, and the words He said were the sweetest music to my ears that I had ever heard because HE said them! *"I want twenty per cent of everything you've got!"* I thought that was His charge for saving me. I was so ignorant of the Bible, I didn't know my salvation was free.

The important thing was that I KNEW it was

the voice of God and I didn't have to wait until three
or four people confirmed it. I heard God and didn't
question it. I didn't wonder for a single minute if it
was the devil or one of his cohorts. I knew instantly
it was God! He didn't yell or holler or threaten me
with dire disaster if I disobeyed. He simply gave me
an opportunity to be an obedient new baby.

I would never have considered disobeying God.
All I knew was that I had heard God and I *wanted* to
obey Him. From the moment of salvation, all I have
ever wanted to do was to obey God.

Let's take a look and see what caused this tremendous turnaround in my giving pattern. Because
I was truly "born again" I became that new creature
in Christ, so I instantly acquired the mind of Christ.
My thinking patterns changed immediately. I didn't
have to work on them, they just changed because I
was a new creation. My mind would never have let
me argue with God over whether or not to be obedient. Jesus never argued with His Father. When we
truly are born again and possess the mind of Christ,
then it will be easy for us to hear and heed that
small, still voice of God.

We possess the mind of Christ. Therefore, we
think exactly the same way Jesus does when it
comes to giving.

What does Jesus think about giving?

Does He think we should hoard our money?

Does He think we should stockpile our money?

Does He think we should hide it?

Does He think we should save it for a rainy day?

Let us take a look in the same book, Luke 6:38

(KJV) and see what it says: *"Give, and it shall be given unto you; good measure, pressed down, and shaken together, and running over, shall men give into your bosom. For with the same measure that ye mete withal it shall be measured to you again."*

Many people think when an offering is taken, that this is a very tacky time; this is a time when we need to count our pennies; this is the time we need to see if we have enough money left to pay all of our bills.

Is this what Jesus said? Does he say hide it, stash it, store it away? No, Jesus has other things to say. He says, *"Give and it shall be given unto you."* Many people don't believe in the giving and receiving system or the sowing and the reaping system. If we possess the mind of Christ, what else can we believe? We must believe exactly the same as He does because He promised in His Word that if we give, we are definitely going to have our needs met...abundantly met...more than we can dream or imagine.

Someone said to me one time, "Don't you think that is really presumptuous to give and expect God to give back to you?" I said, "No, for the very simple reason that when I prayed the sinner's prayer and asked God to save me, I expected God to fulfill His Word." The one thing that God is obligated to do, and wants to do, is to fulfill His Word.

When I confessed my sins, He forgave me. When I confessed with my mouth that Jesus Christ was Lord, He came into my heart and saved me.

I expected Him to do this because He promises it! Therefore, when I give, I anticipate that God will give it back because He said so in His Word. So, because we possess the mind of Christ, we need to anticipate that when we give, when we tithe, and when we make separate offerings over and beyond the tithe, these offerings are going to come back. There is a money-back guarantee that is signed in the New Testament by the Son of the Living God, Jesus, who says when you give you are going to get it back. He doesn't promise a possibility, He promises a reality! Besides our being blessed by His return system, God gets blessed even more because He receives back our willingness to trust Him as our investment advisor.

Possessing the mind of Christ means that we have no doubt in this area. It doesn't say, "Well, I think God will do it for somebody else, but He won't do it for me. Because I possess the mind of Christ, I know that I know that I KNOW that Jesus is going to return it to me.

Now, He may not always return it to me when I think it ought to be returned, but because I possess the mind of Christ, I know that I know that I KNOW that it IS coming back to me. I am not going to change my thinking which would cause me to disagree with Jesus. My thinking is going to line up with His! Jesus knows our hearts and knows whether we selfishly want more or whether we want more for the kingdom of God.

One of the greatest desires of my heart is to get the message across to the Body of Christ about giving to God. I know what it did in my own life when I learned to give, because until God gets your money, He never gets you! I use Luke 6:38 over and over again as I take offerings so that Christians will believe that when you give, you will receive it back.

Every once in a while I say to myself, "Oh, people never get the message of what I'm talking about." I keep preaching on giving to God and wonder occasionally if anybody really hears what I have to say about giving.

As we were eating in our local cafeteria one day, a pastor and his family were eating there, too. As a way of saying "hello" I leaned over their table and said, "I came over to get a bite of your food because I didn't have enough." The pastor's eight-year old son picked up his chocolate pie and gave it to me. I said, "Honey, I wouldn't take your pie, I was only kidding."

He said, "Go ahead and take it, because if you take it, I'll get back a lot more than what is on that plate right now!"

He got the message! He got the message that when you give, it is going to be given back to you, pressed down, shaken together and running all over the place. I said, "Glory to God!" and you could have heard me all over the cafeteria. If no one else sitting under my ministry when I take an offering ever listened and believed what I said, I found one who did. An eight-year-old boy!

We need to believe so fervently that, like the eight-year-old boy, we will be willing to give up the most special part of our dinner knowing that Jesus always gives back more! (And He did. The Lord directed me to take an offering for that little boy which amounted to more than $200.00!)

It is exciting to be a Christian and to recognize what we really do possess because we operate with the mind of Christ. The 16th verse in the 8th chapter of Luke says, *"No one, when he has lit a lamp, covers it with a vessel or puts it under a bed, but sets it on a lampstand, that those who enter may see the light."*

Christians ought to be the most brilliant lights in the world and the loudest blabbermouths in the world. We are going to do exactly what Jesus does because we have His very mind.

We are not going to hide our little light. We are not going to put our head underneath a bushel basket and just hide ourselves away. Because we are like Jesus Christ, we are going to hold our candle up high for the whole world to see! We are going to talk about Jesus wherever we are. We are going to talk about Jesus in airports. We are going to talk about Jesus in the grocery store. We are going to talk about Jesus at the service station.

If we possess the mind of Christ, we are going to be filled with that overwhelming, bubbling desire to see that the whole world gets saved. We are not going to let our light go out! We are going to let it shine brighter and brighter and brighter all the time!

Charles and I have the most marvelous time in the world wherever we go. If it is in an airport, we are singing. Many times we sing in tongues. Many times we just go through airports praising God and having an exciting time. Often people walk up to me and say, "Are you a bride?" just because we look so happy. What a wonderful opportunity this gives us to witness. I say, "Yes, we are the bride of Christ," and we share Jesus with them.

Jesus never hid His light under a bushel. He let His light shine all the time, and as Christians who possess the mind of Christ, we should all do exactly the same thing.

Think of the glory that is going to come to the Father when we all do this. Think how His heart will leap with joy when people begin to look at us and know there is something real super-special about us!

"Then He said to them all, 'If anyone desires to come after Me, let him deny himself, and take up his cross daily, and follow Me. For whoever desires to save his life will lose it, but whoever loses his life for My sake will save it'"(Luke 9:23,24).

Many people say, "Well, my cross is my unsaved husband, that drunken alcoholic. He has been the cross I have carried all these years. He has been an albatross around my neck. He has weighted me down all of these years. He is the cross that I must bear. Because I bear it, I am going to make it into heaven someday."

Some people say, "Oh, the cross I have to bear is this sickness God gave me. Paul had a thorn in the flesh and God never healed him. The cross I am bearing is this sickness that I have which I will never get over. But I will glorify God, because I will continue to love Him in spite of all this."

Beloved, that is not what Jesus is talking about. If we have the mind of Christ, we are going to think exactly the same way He did.

Why did Jesus carry His cross? Because it was something that God had saddled Him with? No, Jesus carried His cross so that He could die willingly to save us. He could have called legions of angels to rescue Him. He chose to suffer and die because He knew the victory that He could then share with you and me.

When we pick up our cross daily, it is to die to self so that our ambitions, our desires, our wants, our longings, and our unquenchable thirst for the lusts and pleasures of this world will be crucified every day.

Remember what Paul said, *"I am crucified with Christ: nevertheless I live; yet not I, but Christ liveth in me: and the life which I now live in the flesh I live by the faith of the Son of God, who loved me, and gave himself for me"* (Galatians 2:20).

Jesus carried His cross to die for us.

We need to carry our cross to die for Him.

This death is a spiritual dying to self every day so that all of these worldly appetites that come up are trodden down. That is the real cross that we bear!

The cross you have to bear is not that unsaved husband. It is not that unsaved wife. It is not those unsaved children who are out there in the world. The cross you need to bear is the cross of dying every day to self and earthly desires.

I was talking to a girl the other night and she asked me to pray that people would stop hurting her feelings. she said, "People are so mean to me, and I get my feelings hurt all of the time."

I said, 'No, I am not going to pray for you." She was startled, so I went on to explain: "What you need to do is to die to self so that people cannot hurt your feelings. Did you ever see a dead man get out of a casket and say to the pastor, 'You hurt my feelings because of what you just said about me?'"

Remember if you are dead to self, you cannot have your feelings hurt. People cannot hurt you by the things they say about you. God's Word tells us that we can expect to get persecuted by people who have the carnal mind which is at enmity with God. We need to die to self every day if we really possess the mind of Christ. We must remember to keep all of these worldly things out of our minds and hearts at all times. Then we need to follow Jesus, which means to do the same things He did on this earth because He says whoever will save his own life will lose it. In other words, if you keep worrying about saving your own life and doing your own thing, you will lose it all. But if you lose your life for Jesus' sake, you will save it. Save what? Your very life! Your eternal life!

You can have something and never really possess it!

Years ago every girl had to have a hope chest before she got married. There were always three things you had to buy first of all. You might have been so poor that you didn't own a pair of decent shoes, but no self-respecting girl who expected to get married could ever get past eighteen years of age and fail to start a set of china, silverware, and crystal.

I started to work at the very height of the

depression. Salaries were unbelievably low. I know what it means not to have anything at all, but one of the first things I ever did after I started working was to buy one piece of china. It took me seven months to pay for it. Then I bought one piece of crystal. It took a year to pay for that! Then came one silver teaspoon. I don't think I ever finished paying for that!

Many girls did go on to fill out the entire set of china, crystal, and silverware, but because all of these things were so expensive, and it had taken so long to pay for them, they were all carefully put away and never used. Those special treasures were taken out and used only at Christmas, Thanksgiving, and Easter. Except to eat from them very carefully, no one except mother could touch them or wash them. The china and crystal were so delicate that there was always fear they might break or the silver would get lost, so all of these expensive items were never used. They sat in breakfronts and china cabinets to be shown off to everyone who came to visit, but to enjoy...NEVER!

You can have the most beautiful china in the world, but it doesn't do you a bit of good if you don't use it. You can have the most delicate crystal and the most ornate silverware. It doesn't do you a bit of good if you don't use it. You own it, yes. But you don't really possess it.

I enjoy everything I own. I use my crystal. I use my china. I use my silver. If something gets broken, first I ask, "Did anybody get hurt?" If everybody is okay, I say, "Hallelujah!" All those worldly things can be replaced.

Because I possess everything I own, I enjoy everything to the hilt. I do not save things for a later date. I buy a new dress and wear it the next day. I use everything I possess and I possess everything I own.

Let's apply this to the mind of Christ. We should not take what we are given at that moment when we are born again and put it up on a shelf and say, "Now, as soon as I get over all of these problems, I am going to take the mind of Christ off the shelf and stick it in my head. Then I'll begin to use what was given to me when I was born again."

Many people say, "I am really going to be a committed Christian as soon as I clean up the mess in my life." Become a committed Christian first and then the mess in your life will get cleaned up without your exerting a lot of effort. Realizing that we possess the mind of Christ and making sure in our spirits that we know that we know that we know that the thinking mechanism we have is actually the mind of Christ, will take us into supernatural realms and out of the realm of the unsaved world.

The world says "You are what you eat." Let's apply that to our Christian lives. What you eat in the natural will either nourish you or harm you. The same is true with the spiritual food you eat. You eat of the Bible and grow upon God's laws or you eat the messages of the world and turn your back on God.

The principles that are listed in the Word of God are extremely important. The Word of God tells you how to operate in today's world.

Jesus said, *"It is written, 'Man shall not live by bread alone, but by every word of God'" (Luke 4:4).*

This doesn't say that you will live by only the portions of scripture that you like or that tickle your fancy. Some portions may be a little hard to listen to because they apply to you and may hit a little close to home.

We need to be nourished by the Word of God and not by physical food alone. What Jesus is saying to me is, "If I possess the mind of Christ, I am going to feed on the Word of God so that I am spiritually alert and awake at all times."

No one can go for a full month without physical food and not feel the effects of food deprivation. Most people can't miss one meal without craving food. We have been trained to eat daily. Our bodies are geared for regular food intake. Our bodies will rebel loudly if we don't give them nourishment.

Some Irishmen recently proved that you can starve to death living only on prayer. They were going to fast until they got their own way. They fasted. They died.

Little babies wouldn't last very long if we didn't accept the responsibility of feeding them. The same thing is true in our spiritual life. God shows us in the physical life what happens to us in the spiritual life if we behave the same way in both areas.

We cannot get along with just an occasional dose of physical food. By the same token, we cannot get along with just an occasional dose of spiritual food. Our spirits will starve.

We need to eat the Word of God every day. There are times when I have an opportunity to read more than I do at other times. There are other times when there are so many time-consuming situations that I don't get to read as much as I would like. I begin to feel spiritually starved if I am not in the Word of God. Give me three, four, or five hours in the Word of God and suddenly I can feel myself coming alive again. The world becomes sunshiny. The world turns warm and rosy and I am sitting right on top of it.

The Word of God inside of you will cause you to grow and grow. You cannot survive as a Christian if you don't continue to feed and feed and feed on the Word of God. One day you will look back and realize that instead of being a crawling, colicky baby Christian, you have become a full grown adult spiritual giant.

Jesus believed the Word. I believe the Word. The more I eat, the more I grow and the more I can utilize the mind of Christ. If I spend more and more time with Him, He spends more and more time with me. If I relinquish my will more and more to Him, He can use me more and more to do His work.

We have been given through salvation, one of the greatest gifts imaginable—the mind of Christ. Let us become so aware of his thinking in all areas and know what His thought patterns are, that we will operate more fully as He desires us to act.

In the following chapters of this book, I have tried to paint a living picture of what our minds will be thinking on subjects which were dear to the heart of Jesus! For three years this book has been a flame burning in my heart. I pray I can pass this flame onto you.

JESUS,...there
Let all hEAVEN
KINgs, king dons

In Momenten Like These

Masterysaver

Lift Your Heart, Lift Your Voice
Receiving the SPIRT of the LORD
Lift your heart, your voice to Him

CHAPTER 2

WHAT DOES JESUS SAY ABOUT BEING "BORN AGAIN"

The expression "born again" has been used very loosely over the last few years and it is easy to see why many people do not actually understand what the term means. When we are born again, we acquire the mind of Christ, and when we truly believe that, only then will our thinking begin to line up with His.

"After dark one night a Jewish religious leader named Nicodemus, a member of the sect of the Pharisees, came for an interview with Jesus. "Sir," he said, "We all know that God has sent you to teach us. Your miracles are proof enough of this." Jesus replied, "With all the earnestness I possess I tell you this: Unless you are born again, you can never get into the Kingdom of God." "Born again!" exclaimed Nicodemus. "What do you mean? How can an old man go back into his mother's womb and be born again?" Jesus replied, "What I am telling you so earnestly is this: Unless one is born of water and the Spirit, he cannot enter the Kingdom of God. Men

*can only reproduce human life, but the Holy Spirit
gives new life from heaven; so don't be surprised at
my statement that you must be born again!" (John
3:1-7 TLB).*

According to Mr. Webster, to be born means to
be brought into life or existence. When we are born
physically, we are brought into life in the world
where we now live. We are at the same time brought
into an existence which will last for a certain
number of years on this earth. When we are born
physically, we undergo a complete change of environment, thinking, acting, and behavior. We go
from a total dependence upon our mother's body to
a dependence upon ourselves.

To be "born again" is in many ways the same
thing as being born the first time. When we are born
again, our behavior changes, our thinking changes,
our actions change and most of the time even our environment changes.

That doesn't mean we have to move out of the
house in which we are living when we are born
again, but our associates (environment) change because we no longer have a desire to go to the places
where we formerly had fun. We no longer enjoy the
people with whom we previously associated, because we possess a new way of thinking and a brand
new set of values in life. And once again we go from
a total dependence of one form—upon our own
brain power, to a total dependence of another
form—upon the power of God.

We are going to think like a new creature.

One Bible translation says that unless a man is

actually or honestly born again, he cannot "see" the kingdom of God, which means that we cannot know the kingdom of God; we cannot even become acquainted with the kingdom of God until we are actually born again by the Spirit of God.

Many people say, "Just saying a prayer makes you born again." While there are many people who have been born again by praying a very simple prayer, unless a change has come into their life and they are actually able to "see" the kingdom of God, or the kingdom of heaven, they are not truly born again.

I vividly remember one of the things I said the first time I ever gave my testimony. "The day I was saved, I believe God opened the windows of heaven and gave me a glimpse of what eternity was all about, and from that day on I have never wanted anything of this earth."

This same experience applies to every born-again believer. When you are truly born again, you "see" the kingdom of God. It is not an actual physical thing, but in the supernatural you see that God has called you to a life which is above and beyond the life you are now experiencing.

Once you have truly seen the kingdom of God, there will never be backsliding or going backwards. There should be no desire to return to the things of this world because you have gotten a glimpse of that perfect hope which is the eternal kingdom of God.

Again, Jesus said in the 5th verse, *"Unless one is born of water and the Spirit, he cannot enter the Kingdom of God."* Because we possess the mind of

Christ, we are going to believe exactly the same way. We are not going to let our carnal mind come into play and say, "Well, I have gone to church all of my life. I have joined my church. I have said the church creed." That has nothing to do with it.

Jesus said, *"Unless a man is born again he cannot see the kingdom of God."* So, because we possess the mind of Christ, we are going to agree one hundred per cent with Jesus that we need to be born again by God's Spirit before we can actually see the kingdom of heaven. But once we have truly been born again by God's Spirit, we *will* be able to see into that spiritual realm with our recreated spirits, or that new man which has risen up within us. We are going to shed the old clothes, the old robes, and we are going to put on the new ones, because we are new creatures in Christ.

II Corinthians 5:17 tells us, *"Therefore, if anyone is in Christ, he is a new creation; old things have passed away; behold, all things have become new."*

We are new creatures in Christ. We are sparkling new lights in the kingdom of God. We are transformed from the old person we used to be into the recreated person that we now are. We should have no desire to do the things we formerly did, because the old things have all passed away and all things have become new. We are going to act like a new creature. We are going to think like a new creature. We are going to speak like a new creature.

To go back into sin, the old way of life, would be the same principle as a grown man saying, "I want to go back into my mother's womb because it was so nice and warm there, and I felt so secure there." Once you are born, you are no longer that little baby floating in the water sack in the womb. You are an individual who is now living in the world, and you can never go back.

The same thing is true of a genuine born-again experience. We have no right, nor should we have a desire to go back to the old things of the sinful world and continue participating in the old way of life. Before I was born again, I smoked, drank, cussed, and told dirty jokes. I certainly was not an example of someone possessing the mind of Christ; however, once I was born again, I became a new creation and the old things passed away!

Over and over I have pondered on one question. Why is it that some people become new creations, and some people don't? Why is it that some people never seem to have trouble in their Christian life, and others never seem to get over the hurdles?

There are many things that all tie together to make the Christian life simple and easy. It all goes back to the genuine born-again experience. Being born again is not an emotional experience where we cry and are drained emotionally, only to get up from an altar and live the same way we did previously.

We know that an individual cannot come to Jesus unless the Spirit of God draws him, but once the Spirit draws him, the responsibility for the effectiveness of the born-again experience rests upon the person himself. Salvation is not a decision of the emotions. Salvation is a decision of the will. Emotions are often the result of a genuine born-again experience, but are not always indicative of a genuine experience.

Genuine salvation comes from our own will. Until we can honestly say, I WILL to follow after Jesus; I WILL to be obedient to God; I WILL to walk away from sin; I WILL to be the person that God wants me to be, our salvation can be wishy-washy and on-again, off-again.

When we truly make this decision of our will, we have done our part; then Jesus does His part. The Spirit of Jesus merges with or comes into our spirit. We are conceived by the Holy Spirit; God plants His Seed (Jesus), His life, into our spirits, and from that Seed, Jesus, we are born spiritually. Romans 8:9 (TLB) says, *"...And remember that if anyone doesn't have the Spirit of Christ living in him, he is not a Christian at all."*

The glorious day that Jesus became my Savior and Lord, I WILLED to follow Him. I looked up to God and said, "God, I'll make a deal with you. I'll give you ALL of me for ALL of you!"

God took me up on the deal I offered him, and even though I got the best of the "deal", the decision of my own intellect and mind has kept me on the Christian road for all these years without ever backsliding, without ever questioning or doubting God, without ever wondering if the Christian life really worked, and without ever wanting to return to the old life.

I made a decision that was not forced by emotions, a song, or a religious atmosphere. It was a decision that I had clearly thought about for months while I was attending a Bible preaching church. It was a decision that had been made before I went to church on a particular Sunday morning. I looked at what the devil had to offer and at what God had to offer. I liked God's offer much better, so with my own free will, I deliberately chose to follow God.

Throughout His lifetime, Jesus always chose to follow God's will for His life. Even at the cross, He never questioned that God's will would override any human emotions He might have.

There is always a delicate balance between "works" and "grace" because works are insufficient to secure salvation. Please do not feel that I am trying to say that you can earn your way into heaven, because I tried that for years via the tuna fish and cream cheese sandwich bit and washing dishes in the church basement after church dinners. It doesn't work. We know that, *"For by grace you have been saved through faith, and that not of yourselves; it is the gift of God, not of works, lest anyone should boast. For we are His workmanship, created in Christ Jesus for good works, which God prepared beforehand that we should walk in them"* (Ephesians 2:8-10). Good works will follow the believer, but the works alone won't save the unbeliever.

Every day we are confronted with opportunities to WILL to be obedient to God, or to WILL to be disobedient. Every action in which we are involved is an opportunity to do what God wants us to, or an occasion to make a decision not to obey Him. Where we go, what we listen to, what we read, what we watch, what we hear, what we see is a daily opportunity for us to be obedient to what God tells us in His Word. That is why when a person has a genuine born-again experience, it is easy for him to be obedient to God, because he possesses the mind of Christ and will want to do the same things Jesus did. Jesus never even considered disobeying His Father. He had the mind of God. When we follow Jesus with all our hearts, we will have the mind of God.

If we have not WILLED to make a complete and total commitment of our lives, and it is definitely a decision of our own WILL, we are going to have problems all the way throughout our Christian life because there is no way we can walk with one foot in the Spirit and the other foot in the devil's territory.

A beautiful scripture that puzzled me for years was recently made plain by the Holy Spirit and it fits in so perfectly with what Jesus thinks about being born again.

Matthew 9:16,17 says: *"No one puts a piece of unshrunk cloth on an old garment; for the patch pulls away from the garment, and the tear is made worse. Nor do people put new wine into old wineskins, or else the wineskins break, the wine is spilled, and the wineskins are ruined. But they put new wine into new wineskins, and both are preserved."*

The second verse is the verse that pertains to being the new creature in Christ when we are truly born again. It plainly shows the ridiculousness and futility of trying to live a Christian life while still living in sin. You cannot cram the new birth experience into a life that is still interested in the things of the flesh, because the penalty is that it will burst at the seams and the end result will be worse than your life was in the beginning.

When you put the new wine, new life (which is the new birth experience) into your life, it has to be put into a vessel that is clean and pure. You may say, "Well, when I asked God to forgive my sins, didn't He forgive them?" Yes, He did, but if you WILL to go your own way and you WILL to do your own thing, your temple is going to be cluttered up again immediately with sin, and the new wine (or the new birth experience) and the old wineskins (or the old life) are both ruined and you are worse off than before. However, when you WILL to be a new creature in Christ and you WILL to be a new creature in your physical being, then BOTH are preserved.

It is impossible to be truly born again without a commitment of your will to God and a decision to stop following after the dictates of your flesh. The most miserable people in the world are those who have said a sinner's prayer and then have gone back to their old way of living. The miserable, pathetic church-goer who says, "I just can't give up cigarettes because I still like to smoke" is far more miserable than the individual who has never said a sinner's prayer, but just goes on enjoying being a sinner.

It is just as hard to be a half-way Christian as it is to try to make a new patch hold on an old pair of jeans. You put new material on top, but the threads underneath are so worn out they won't hold the thread of the new one.

Colossians 3:23 tells us one of the easiest ways

to enjoy Christianity to its fullest, *"And whatever you do, do it heartily, as to the Lord and not to men."* *"Do it heartily"* means that we should never be half-hearted in anything we do for the Lord. Jesus tells us in Revelation what's going to happen to us if we are. *"I know your works, that you are neither cold nor hot. I could wish you were cold or hot. So then, because you are lukewarm and neither cold nor hot, I will spew you out of My mouth"* (Revelations 3:15,16).

Because we possess the mind of Christ, let's get red hot, on-fire for the Lord, because that was Jesus all the way. Jesus said unless we were born again, we could never get into the kingdom of God, so let's make sure that we are truly a new creature in Christ by making that decision with our will to stop playing around and really get serious with God right now.

Let's say a prayer together to make sure we really are born again because you WILL to be a Christian!

Father, I'm not interested in going to hell. I want to go to heaven, but I am always full of tacky things in my life. I ask You to forgive me and wash me in the precious blood of Jesus. Lord Jesus, with my mind, my intellect and my will, I invite You to come into my heart and to make me the kind of person You want me to be. I WILL to follow YOU. I WILL to live above sin. I WILL to be obedient in everything You tell me to do. I WILL to serve You. I WILL to make a complete commitment of my life to You right now. Thank You for saving me and hear-

ing my prayer.

Something happened to you in that split second of time when you were born again by the Spirit of God. When we fully realize what actually happens to us in that moment, it should be the most awe-inspiring thing that ever occurs in our life.

Many of us said a little sinner's prayer in the past, but since we did not have any teaching up to that point, we didn't understand what really happened to us. Because the world doesn't teach us the things of God, the carnal mind is at enmity with God and cannot understand the things of the Spirit.

In one split second, we jump from a sinners' world with a natural mind into the spirit world with all the supernatural activities of God. In other words, God still operates through us as human beings but He does it in such a super way that it becomes a supernatural way.

There is a supernatural thing that takes place within us when we are born again. We no longer belong to the devil. We belong to God. We no longer operate with the mind of a sinner because we have been given the mind of Christ. Now we have to learn to utilize the wisdom of Jesus and thus operate with His mind in control

God doesn't say, "After you have been saved six months, I'll give you the mind of Christ."

No, when you are born again, you become a new creature. At that very moment, even though you may not act like it or feel like it, you really are a new creature with the mind of Christ.

Some people have a very dramatic experience.

They understand and know they are a new person with a new chance at life. Others do not. It becomes a struggle until we actually learn that we just have to receive and act on what is given to us.

Let me give you a simple example of what I mean. I doubt if you remember when you were born in your natural life. Something very dramatic happened to you on that day when you actually became a separate person operating independently of your mother. Until that time you were depending upon the food and the strength and the nourishment in your mother's body to give you the necessary things to grow.

Once you entered the world and that umbilical cord was cut, a drastic change took place. No longer could you depend on your mother in the same involuntary way as before. You had to look to outside sources for nourishment. No longer did you have all of your lifegiving substance flow into your body through the umbilical cord.

Suddenly, you became a little entity all by yourself. Probably all you did was to cry, scream, holler and sleep in between meals. Oh, you could wiggle your hands and feet, but your productive activity was very limited.

I like to compare an infant's development with the Christian life. The moment you are born again, that umbilical cord to the devil is cut. You have been fed by the devil up until the time you are born again. Once that cord is cut, he no longer can feed you his lies. You have become a separate and a special person in the kingdom of God.

Many people think they should be spiritual giants and fully mature right off the bat. Rarely does that happen. I have never known a child who came out of his mother's womb walking and leaping and praising God. When you're born again, it is the same growing-up principle that applies to your physical development.

There are some things which are natural for us to do as a baby. Crying is a natural reflex a baby uses to communicate with the world. They are uncomfortable in one of many ways—they are wet, cold, hot or hungry. As soon as their needs are met, they go off to sleep.

But what happens if they have gotten the wrong food? Have you ever heard of colic? Many babies have it at one time or another. But do you know what? They all grow out of it.

Compare this to the Christian life. We talk, listen, read, eat and sleep as baby Christians. But what happens if we don't get enough to eat? Perhaps we eat something that we aren't able to digest. Perhaps we eat the wrong food and get sick. I call this "Christian colic."

Sometimes things get so complicated that we think, "Oh, I can't understand this. I don't understand this so I can't possibly live the Christian life."

All you really have is a case of Christian colic and you need to keep on a bit further. You'll get over that Christian colic. No child ever grew up into his adult years continuing to have colic and rare is the child who ever has it after they reach two years of age.

The same thing should be true in our Christian life. As baby Christians, maybe we are entitled to a little Christian colic once in awhile when we are first born again by the Spirit of God. However, we need to get over it and go on in the Lord growing and reaching out to others. We no longer should be laying there in our comfortable baby beds screaming, hollering, kicking and fussing.

Just as babies practice walking, we must practice the spiritual laws God has given us. Babies trip, fall down and bruise their knees as well as their noses as they learn. But they don't stay down. Young children see the exciting things adults are doing and are determined to act like the "big people" do.

Baby Christians have to do the same thing. Get your eyes on Jesus and know you possess His mind. You may fall down, make mistakes, bruise your ego and have your nose bent, but you have been given all the tools necessary to grow and develop in the Christian life. Just as in human development however, if you don't exercise your arms, legs, and voice, they will shrivel, die and be useless. Get busy and exercise!

CHAPTER THREE

WHAT DOES JESUS SAY ABOUT "CHRIST IN YOU, THE HOPE OF GLORY"

The book of John probably is the greatest of all of the gospels in line with what Paul preached, *"Christ in you, the hope of glory."* Jesus said some tremendous things about being the true vine and the Father the true vinedresser in the 15th chapter of John.

"Every branch in Me that does not bear fruit He takes away...Abide in Me and I in you." It's a two-way proposition. We abide *in* Him, and He abides *in* us! I looked up the word *abide,* and it means "to go into". To go into something means to be so wholly submerged that there is no part of you left over at all.

Jesus said, *"Abide in Me and I in you. As the branch cannot bear fruit of itself, unless it abides in the vine, neither can you, unless you abide in Me"* (John 15:4).

Jesus is saying to us that if we do not "abide" in Him, we cannot have the fruit and the fruitfulness

He wants us to have. He said, *"If we abide in Him"*, or if we *"go into Him"* so totally and so completely that our own self nature wholly disappears, then we can have much fruit. Without Him we can have nothing.

He goes on to say, *"If anyone does not abide in Me, he is cast out as a branch and is withered; and they gather them and throw them into the fire, and they are burned."* But verse 7 in that chapter says some powerful words, *"If you abide in Me,"* (go into Me) *"and My words abide in you"* (go into you) *"you will ask what you desire, and it shall be done for you."*

What a promise of God! Anything and everything we want will be done, will be accomplished, will be given if we just so much as desire it, if we will just so completely immerse ourselves in Him and "go into Him" that there will be absolutely no recognition of what we used to be before we became a Christian .

In verse 9 Jesus said, *"As the Father loved Me, I also have loved you; abide in My love. If you keep My commandments, you will abide in My love, just as I have kept My Father's commandments and abide in His love."* He wants us to "go into" His love so we will experience in our own lives a love that is above and beyond anything we would ever be able or capable of doing in the natural. The reason He wants us to do that is so His joy may remain in us; so we will have His joy operating at top speed within us at all times.

One time when T.L. and Daisy Osborn were at

our home, we were talking about *"Christ in you, the hope of glory."* I mentioned to T.L. that the first thing I ever learned as a brand new baby Christian was that Jesus Christ lived IN me. He was surprised that it was so clear to me so quickly because when he was a young minister and preached that Jesus lived in him, many thought he was a heretic. Everyone ought to understand that Jesus actually does live in us.

If we can get to the point where we totally and completely and positively believe that Jesus is living inside of us, walking through our feet, working through our hands, and speaking through our lips, it will do a lot to eliminate the problems that develop sometimes in our Christian life just because we don't understand the simple principle of *"Christ in you, the hope of glory"* and of abiding in Him in all of His glory and His power and His majesty.

It is such an incredible and absolutely overwhelming thought to realize that we actually have the ability of God within us because Jesus said, *"All authority—all power of rule—in heaven and on earth has been given to Me"* (Matthew 28:18 Amplified), and then Jesus turned right around and said to us, *"Behold! I have given you authority and power to trample upon serpents and scorpions, and (physical and mental strength and ability) over all the power that the enemy (possesses), and nothing shall in any way harm you"* (Luke 10:19 Amplified).

Sometimes it is difficult to describe the actual experience of knowing that you know that you know that Jesus Christ is living big inside of you, to walk in that faith and to believe in the knowledge that Jesus is actually living there. This gives you unlimited power. We should never preach the gospel if we cannot DO the gospel. If we really believe Jesus lives inside of us, then we ought to be able to do everything that was done in the Bible.

Christians live far below the level of where God wants us to live. We seek for the lesser things, we are satisfied with the lesser things and we fail to reach up and to reach out into those higher heights of glory into the world of the unknown, into the world of the unseen, into the world that has never really been tampered with.

God wants us to reach out to a new world. He wants us all to operate in the supernatural. When we really believe Jesus Christ is living in and through us in the power of the Holy Spirit, we will be loaded with *"enteos"*, which means enthusiasm. It means God within. When you have Jesus Christ living in you, you are going to be enthusiastic. God within equals enthusiasm. I have never known anyone who could prove to me that they were really a Christian if they weren't excited about Jesus and what He has done in their lives. I have never seen a dead-pan Christian. I have seen a lot of "dead-pan" people, but never a dead-pan Christian.

What are we going to be enthusiastic about? If Jesus lives within, we're going to be enthusiastic about our salvation. The very first thing that you are going to be enthusiastic about is the fact that Jesus Christ is living IN you. If you are truly saved, you will be excited about what Jesus has done in your life. The reason I am so wild and excited all of the time is that I let Jesus do something in my life. Did you notice that I said, "I let Him"? God never forces you to do a thing.

I fell so madly in love with Jesus that down the drain went the cigarettes, down the drain went the alcohol, down the drain went all of those horrible habits that I had before I got saved. I am excited about salvation because salvation gave me the power to be the kind of person God wanted me to be instead of the kind of woman the devil wanted me to be. Many people hang onto the devil even after they think they are saved because they are not willing to let God make those changes in their lives which need to be made. I can guarantee you that any change God wants to make within us is for the better. Everything He does is an improvement in our lives!

Many people say, "Oh, I have to give up this." No, you don't have to give up a thing. He lifts you above the desire to do the things you did before you got saved. That is why I am so excited about salvation. It gave me a new outlook. I became a new creation. I became a new creature. My mind was renewed. No longer did I have the old dirty, filthy mind that I had before I got saved. That is why I am so excited about salvation, because Jesus Christ living within you and me makes us bubble up and just burst with excitement over what He has done for us.

We are also going to be excited about healing the sick. We are not only going to be excited, we are going to be super-excited!

Before I received the baptism with the Holy Spirit, something happened that I will never forget. A man walked up to me in St. Petersburg, Florida, and said, "God has given you the gift of healing. Why don't you use it?" Before I had a chance to open my mouth, he just plain disappeared right in front of my eyes. I wonder if it was an angel? Whoever it was, I have never forgotten that very special moment when someone said, "You have the gift of healing." That stayed in my mind, and I thought, "Wow! Could that ever happen to me?"

Especially during the holiday season, I look at some of the unhappy faces of people in the grocery store, in the shopping center and in the mall. These people are frantically racing around trying to find the answer to life. Running, running, running, running, looking, looking, looking! Why? Because they have not yet found the answer to life. They haven't found that Christ in you is the only true source of glory! We don't have to be running, running, running constantly trying to find the answer. We've got it! That's why we can be enthusiastic, because God within us makes it possible.

When I got saved, Jesus opened my mouth, and I haven't shut it since! And I don't intend to shut it, because it is that *"enteos"* within me that makes it impossible to talk about anything else but Jesus.

Jesus in us will allow us to become the new creature that we are promised. We are not going to be digging up the garbage of the past saying, "Oh, but I had all these awful things in the past." Who cares! Quit bragging about your past. Start talking about who you are now and what Jesus did for you.

We are going to believe in our new life, and we are going to believe in the new creation.

We are not going to concentrate on problems. We are not going to talk about them, because talking about problems make them grow and grow, and grow and grow! Pretty soon you are overwhelmed by problems. Get your mind off of the problems and on the answer. When you begin thinking about Jesus, about God, and about what God has done in your life, your problems are just going to slip away and disappear, and they are going to be as though they never were.

The Jesus in us has a hungering for the Word of God. The more we get into God's Word, the more we are going to discover that as we begin to grow, we begin to rise, and rise, and rise. Our problems don't rise with us. The problems stay way down there. But as we rise, we get further and further away from our problems, until suddenly they are so insignificant we can't see them any more.

One of the best examples I know of in this area happens when you ride in a plane. When you first take off from the airport, you look out the window and you can see everything plainly and in clear detail, but the higher the plane goes, the smaller the houses become as you begin to rise higher and higher above them.

The same thing is true with your spiritual life. As you begin to go into those spiritual realms, the problems get smaller and smaller, and smaller until suddenly they are so little you cannot see them any more.

"Christ in you, the hope of glory" is going to make us excited about the power of God to overcome in every area in our life!

CHAPTER FOUR

WHAT DOES JESUS SAY ABOUT "REPENTANCE"

Charles and I are blessed to have a ministry that goes around the world. It is an international ministry which not only touches the lives of people in the United States, but also in many other countries. As a result we receive mail from people in diverse cultural, social, economic and ethnic backgrounds.

Surprisingly, the contents of these letters say the same thing. A letter sent from a city here in the United States will be similar to a letter sent from a city in Europe.

After a while we began to notice a pattern in the needs expressed by people in their letters and discovered that specific spiritual problems are not confined to any particular locale. One problem in particular is mentioned repeatedly all over the world. It seems that people everywhere are struggling and failing in their attempts to live a Christian life. But as far as we can determine from their mail, these people are tripping over "step one" of living an overcoming, victorious, fulfilled life as a believer.

That step is repentance.

Recently, I read a letter from a lady in Queensland, Australia, that was amazingly similar to a letter I had just read from someone in Nigeria. Another letter from a man in Indianapolis, Indiana was almost the same. They were all saying, "I *want* to love God and I *want* to walk the Christian way. I am *trying* to lead a good moral life — but what is the matter with me?" In each case the writer desperately wanted to serve God but their life seemed empty and cold, and they could not see the manifestation of God in their personal situation. Each one literally broke my heart.   Each letter also had another similarity. Each of them wrote that they had said the sinner's prayer many times (one even wrote that she had prayed it about fifty times), but had not seen any results from their prayers. Their lives seemed to just go on as before with no real life, no hungering for the Word of God or the things of God, and they were as defeated as they had been before the prayers.

Matthew 4:17 says, *"From that time Jesus began to preach and to say, 'REPENT, for the kingdom of heaven is at hand.'"* There is the important step the people from Australia, Nigeria and Indianapolis — and all over the world — have missed in entering into the type of Christian life the Word of God exemplifies.

Mark 1:14 says the same thing. It states, *"Now after John was put in prison, Jesus came to Galilee, preaching the gospel of the kingdom of God, and saying, 'The time is fulfilled, and the kingdom of*

God is at hand. Repent, and believe in the gospel.'"
Once again the Word of God instructs us in the process of spiritual birth. Not only did Jesus say to *repent,* but also to *believe.*

Webster's dictionary defines repentance as, "To feel pain, sorrow, or regret for something that one has done, or left undone; to be conscience stricken or contrite; to change one's mind about some past action, intention in consequence, or regret or dissatisfaction." It goes on to say that in theology it means, "To feel sorrow for sin as leads to amendment of one's ways, to be penitent."

Now I want to show you what the Word of God says about repentance. Researching the word repentance in Hebrew and Greek, I found there are eight words describing repentance. These eight words, four in Hebrew and four in Greek, give us the total picture of true Bible repentance. There are different places in scripture where each of these meanings was used for a specific purpose.

Going back to the scripture reference used earlier, Jesus said to *"Repent, for the kingdom of God is at hand"*, and to *"Repent and believe."* The first repent in Hebrew is *"nacham"* which means to sigh or to breathe strongly or to be sorry. In this type of repentance one is sorry for something he has done. For example, if you put your life's savings in a particular stock which had shown tremendous gain, only to suddenly go right down to the bottom and be worthless, you would be very sorry. You would regret putting all your money into what turned out to be a bad investment. This is a form of repentance, by avoid-

ing something because you have found out by experience that it wasn't a wise thing to do.

Another Hebrew word for repentance is
"shuwb" which means to turn back. It means not re-
peating something because you have learned that
there is a consequence to it, such as touching a hot
stove. Any young child can testify to that kind of repentance. Once he has been burned, he will be careful to avoid contact with the flame so it won't happen again.

The third Hebrew word for repentance,
"nocham", is particularly interesting. It means to
regret rather than repent. The sorrow is connected
with being found out rather than for committing the
sin.

An excellent example of *"nocham"* is a person
who robs a bank. If they successfully accomplished
the robbery, made a fast getaway, leaving no finger-
prints or identification behind and lived their life in
prosperity to the end of their days, there would be
no repentance.

BUT—if they were caught and sent to prison,
they would "regret" their action. This is proven by
the fact that many prisoners repeat their crime as
soon as they are released, which indicates no repentance or turning away, but a desire to do it again and
not get caught!

Compassion is the meaning of the fourth Hebrew word for repentance. It is *"nichum"* and is an
emotional concern for other people. When we acquire the nature of God, because we have been
created in the very image of God, we should acquire

the compassion of Jesus. But just because you feel sorry for someone else does not mean you truly repent for what you have done in *your* life. There are a lot or organizations which are not Christian, but operate out of compassion for other people. Many collect food and clothing and give away Christmas baskets and toys because of their compassion. That type of compassion is admirable, but it is not repentance.

In the Greek language the word *"metanoa"* means to change your mind for the better or to change your attitude toward sin. This is strictly a mental change of mind. That is "sense" knowledge which says, "I am going to straighten up my life. It is not good for me to be smoking cigarettes, because the Surgeon General's report said it could be harmful, so I am going to quit smoking." It means to change your own mind.

Someone who is poor might say, "I have lived in poverty long enough. I don't like poverty, so I am going to be something different from now on. I am going to make some money for myself."

I said that myself many, many years ago before I ever got saved. I was raised in abject poverty, and somewhere along the line, I decided I was going to be rich. It didn't matter how long or how hard I had to work, I was going to get some money. From the time I was seventeen years old I worked at least two jobs at a time, sometimes 12,14,16 or even 18 hours a day for one reason: *I wanted money.* I had changed my mind about being poor and was willing to work and do everything required to rise above my poverty. But that kind of repentance has nothing to do with true repentance which totally changes your life.

The second Greek word for repentance is "*metamelomai*" which is to regret the consequence of sin, not the cause of sin. This type of repentance was clearly illustrated to Charles and me not too long ago.

We received a frantic telephone call from a young man we had known for several years. The young man was in jail. "Please, come and get me out," he pleaded.

"What did you do to get arrested?" I asked.

"Nothing," he replied. "My car broke down on the highway and I was trying to repair it when the police came by and began to accuse me of doing something illegal. Now, they have put me in jail and won't even let me post bond."

We were very concerned about the young man, but his explanation about his arrest didn't make much sense. Policemen don't indiscriminately arrest people without a reason. And although we wanted to help the young man, we did not have the freedom from the Holy Spirit to rush down to jail and try to get the young man out.

God gives you connections when you need connections and keeps you from going off the deep end to help someone who perhaps should not be helped at that particular time. Through a friend in the police department, we discovered that the young man was not innocently hauled into jail as he had claimed, but was charged with being caught in a homosexual act. The young man had lied to us just to use us to get him out of jail. He was not sorry at all for what he had done, but was sorry he had been caught. He wanted a quick, easy way out of the situation.

This seems to be common, we have noticed, in homosexual behavior. It is sometimes difficult for homosexuals to totally turn around and be changed into the image of God, becuase they only regret the *consequences* of their sin. They regret the fact that they are found out, but deep down in their hearts they do not regret the act itself. That is because they have never really genuinely repented of the sin of homosexuality in their lives.

This type of repentance—being sorry only for the consequence of sin—also applies to other areas. For example, speeding. Have you ever gotten a ticket for going over the speed limit? Did it make you more conscious of the law and help you stay within the allowable speed?

I was stopped once for rushing through a stop sign. When the policeman pulled up alongside the car, I realized instantly why I was being stopped. "I didn't come to a dead stop at that stop sign, did I?" I confessed as he walked over to my car. He laughed heartily at my total honesty. In fact, he didn't even write me a ticket because I was sincerely sorry for what I had done. Even to this day when I come to a stop sign, I totally stop, pray in tongues, and proceed cautiously. My repentance for failure to abide by the law that says come to a complete stop at a stop sign caused me to change my ways.

There are some people I know (I'm sure you can

recall some, too) who have had one speeding ticket right after the other. That says, "I am only sorry I got caught. I am only sorry I had to pay big, big fines because I was going 85 miles an hour in a 55 mile per hour speed zone." That is not repentance. Instead, that person becomes more careful in watching his rear view mirror than watching his speed. No Christian should ever get a speeding ticket. And if he does, it should make him repentant enough to change his driving habits to comply with local, state and federal laws.

God's Word tells us to obey the law. I don't have to worry about checking the rear view mirror; all I have to be concerned with is God, and He knows whether I am going 55 miles an hour or not. Some people think I don't drive fast enough, that I am slow. It takes me a little longer to get there, but I get there. God has angels around my car. Hallelujah! The angels get off when you drive over 55 miles an hour, so I would rather drive the speed limit and make sure they stay there!

What keeps most people walking the "straight and narrow"? Sometimes they walk that way not just because they want to, but because they are afraid of the consequences if they don't. Many people would go out and rob a bank if they thought they could get away with it. Many would steal from stores if they knew no one would find out. Occasionally, it is reported in the newspapers that someone has embezzled money from a company or bank, or misappropriated funds in some other way. When they are found out, the people who have committed

these deeds are sorry—not for the deed itself, but for
the fact they were discovered.

As Christians we should always be meticu-
lously honest in all business dealings, not because
we *have* to, but because we *want* to. The Holy Spirit
within us will act as an umpire to make sure that
when we have acted discreditably, we can ask for
forgiveness, correct our action and get back on
course.

In the two scriptures I referred to earlier, the
word for repentance that Jesus used was the word
"metanoia" which means a real change of mind, an
attitude toward sin, not merely the consequences of
it. In other words, one might sincerely say, "Oh,
God, I am sorry I said this or did that."

This matter of true repentance—or lack of true
repentance—is evidenced in the many letters
Charles and I receive. People say that their lives are
defeated, but they don't really know why. They
think the promises of God don't work in their lives.
They ask but they don't receive. They give but they
don't prosper. "Why?" they wonder. God has clearly
shown me that the reason people are defeated, and
the promises of God seemingly don't work in their
lives, is because *they do not truly repent.*

Many people say the sinner's prayer, but it stops
right there. The Word of God says, *"For godly sorrow worketh repentance to salvation"* (II Corinthians 7:10 KJV). I believe we have had many defeated Christians because they never really under-
stood what Jesus meant when He said, *"Repent"*. He
meant to turn your back on what you were doing.

This isn't merely giving something up to be a Christian. I never gave up one single thing. I was the wildest smoker, drinker, "cusser," and dirty joke teller you ever saw until I met Jesus as Lord and Savior.

Being a Christian doesn't mean you *have* to give things up; it means you *get* to! You *get* to give up all those destructive habits and life styles which will hurt your life. And you *get* to give up that old, dead spirit man who is condemned to eternal damnation.

Many of you might look at me and find it hard to believe that before 1965 I was a wild sinner. My vocabulary would have shocked you. But a peculiar thing happened in my life. I did not say the sinner's prayer when I first heard the third chapter of John. I heard it and realized that I was not really born again. I *thought* I was a Christian. I went to church on Sundays. And even though I lived like the devil the rest of the week, smoking, drinking and cursing; I thought going to church made me a Christian. What a shock it was to find out I had not really been born again!

But even though I realized I was not really saved, I was reluctant to make a decision. I continued to smoke, drink and live my own life as I always had. But the Spirit of God continued to convict me and show me I was a sinner. About nine months later I cried out, "Oh, God, have mercy on me, a sinner!"

That day, God reached down and saved me. Not only had I called on God for mercy, but beneath the voice that asked for help was a heart that was broken and contrite. When God saved me, I *knew* I was saved. In fact, I was so euphoric that for about two days I didn't even know who I was! But I knew Jesus Christ was living in my heart! I remembered thinking, "He's in there—He's in there!" Jesus was in my heart, so I slammed the door, locked it, and threw away the key and said, "Jesus, don't you ever get out of there!"

The very second I said that, my life began to change, not mildly, but drastically! I acquired a hungering for the Word of God and was sure that all Bibles would be confiscated before I finished reading the book which had laid on a table in my house for such a long time untouched by human hands! I wanted to find out everything God had to say. I could never get enough of God!

There was something special about nighttime. Maybe it was because I was away from the hustle and bustle of my printing company, away from the telephones—away from people—away from anything that would destroy the intimate relationship I was developing with God.

It seemed I would be engulfed in His love when I snuggled down into bed and turned the lights off. It was "Just you and me, Lord!" I would savor every precious minute of the love-relationship we were developing. My heart and soul cried out to please Him.

Night after night a pattern seemed to be developing. I began to remember all the things I had done from "little bitty on". I remembered the penny I stole from my mother. I said, "Oh, God, I am sorry for that."

I was genuinely sorry. I wasn't sorry that I got caught. I was sorry I had sinned against God. While I do not think it is necessary for everyone to do this, I went back over my entire life and over and over again the same thing would happen. I would begin to sob, I would cry, and cry and cry. Sometimes I would cry for two or three hours and couldn't even remember what I was crying about.

It was not a sad cry of remembering things like, "I lost my mother. I lost my father. I lost my husband before I was 35 years old." It was not that kind of a cry I cried on each of those occasions. It was a cry that was actually a "glad" cry. Somehow or other, I seemed to be sobbing from the innermost depths of my heart. I couldn't figure out what I was crying about, and yet, when I finished and finally fell a-sleep, I felt good. My body felt good, my soul felt good, and I just felt good all over. The next morning I would think, "I can't stay awake every night cry-ing, so tonight I'll go right to sleep."

But when night came and I went to bed and began to love God and talk to Him in the quietness of the darkness, because that is always such a beau-tiful time to talk with God, I discovered I was doing the same thing over and over again.

I would say, "Oh, God, I love you. Thank you for saving me. Thank you for forgiving me of all my sins. Oh, God, I am truly and sincerely sorry for every-thing wrong I have ever done. Then I would begin to think of a lot more things, and I would start all over again. I am sure I told God about things that He didn't even think were a sin anyway, but I believe I thought of everything I had ever done in my entire life.

I went to school in Chicago and the school had far more blacks than whites. I remember my dancing partner was a black boy and I hated him and everybody that made me dance with that little black boy. I had not thought of that in forty years, yet here I was saying, "God, forgive me, I was not nice to that little boy. I am so sorry."

I thought of the most peculiar things you could ever imagine. But in my heart, I was genuinely sorry for anything and everything I had ever done from the day I was born until the day I got saved. It's amazing what the Holy Spirit brings back to your mind when you are truly repentant. I didn't know then what was happening to me in these nightly engagements I had with God, but today I know it was the Holy Spirit tears that were cleansing me with godly sorrow for everything I had ever done against God!

I do not believe it is necessary for everybody to smell the garbage in their life before they were saved. In my case, I can see it was necessary that I bring it out to myself, because my biggest problem was that I had difficulty telling God I was a sinner. When He finally did show me and convince me that I was a sinner, I began to see all the things I had done in my life and had refused to admit they were sin.

When you are open to God, the Holy Spirit will bring to your remembrance many things. Each night I would remember something else, as I was putting a searchlight into my innermost being. Once again, my body would be torn with sobs. It was a cry from the very depths of my heart as I sobbed and sobbed telling God how sorry I was.

That same type of repentance may not have happened to you, but I believe that churches need to preach more about repentance, because getting "saved" doesn't mean just saying a sinner's prayer. You will discover that you will walk the Christian road like God wants you to walk if there is true repentance in your heart. The condemnation most people have in their Christian life is because they have not truly repented and turned the opposite direction.

The next most important thing is to go on and forget your past. We need to realize that our sins have not only been forgiven by God, but forgotten as well, because He buries them in the deepest sea, never to be remembered again. We need to accept the forgiveness of God in our life, and go on from there.

God is not going to throw you out for some little sin you committed after you got saved. The minute you do something wrong, ask His forgiveness right then and there and never do it again. We don't need to worry unless we keep on doing the same thing over and over again. I John 1:9 says, *"If we confess our sins, He is faithful and just to forgive us and to cleanse us of all unrighteousness."*

The Amplified Bible states that verse this way: *"If we [freely] admit that we have sinned and confess our sins, He is faithful and just [true to His own nature and promises] and will forgive our sins (dismiss*

*our lawlessness) and continuously cleanse us from
all unrighteousness—everything not in conformity
to His will in purpose, thought and action."*

One of the things which amazes me about God is
that if you said a sinner's prayer right now, and then
five minutes later remembered some atrocious sin
you had committed and said, "Oh, God, did you forgive me for that awful sin I committed 37 years
ago?" God would say, "What sin?" because He
doesn't even remember.

After I was saved, I cried for two or three
months every night. All the nasty things I had ever
said to anyone came back to my mind. I remember
that I lied to a teacher when I was in the fourth
grade. I thought to myself, "Oh, God, that was such
a little lie." Then I realized there is no such thing as
a little lie. All lies are BIG lies. I said, "Oh, God, I am
sorry for that. I am sorry because I was the leader in
the class, and I told a lie to the teacher." Then there
would come those buckets of tears, the sobbing that
racked my body, and then finally the peace of God!

What does repentance really mean? It means
turning away, turning as fast as you can in the other
direction, and going as fast as you can go away from
sin.

Many people do not want to give up sin because
they are not really sorry they sinned. Girls come to
me over and over again when we are on the road and
say something like this: "I want to say a sinner's
prayer again. I want to ask God to forgive me. I went
to bed with a boy last night and I knew I shouldn't
have done it."

I say, "Did you ever do it before?"

Their answer is stereotyped: "Oh, yes, every Saturday night, every Wednesday night, too, and then Tuesday and Thursday with another guy, but I want to say a sinner's prayer again."

I guarantee you that kind of a person will be back at the altar the next Sunday because she will do the same thing all over again. Why? Because that individual was not genuinely sorry. The minute your heart really and truly repents, and you say, "Oh, God, I am sorry. I turn my back on that, and I will never do it again", that is the day when godly sorrow will come into your heart. And godly sorrow is the most joyful experience in the world because it leads to your eventual happiness in the Lord. I believe the reason I am so happy and free today is because of the repentance that came into my life. A repentance that said, "God, I will never, never do it again."

When I smoked my last cigarette, there was never a question of whether or not I was going to smoke again. I was sorry I had degraded the holy temple of God. Your body is definitely the holy temple of God, according to His Word. I was so sorry because I could see those black lungs in my body full of "goop", and I was sorry I had ever done such a thing to God's temple. I believe that is the reason I have never been tempted by a cigarette from the day I was set free.

The same thing is true of alcohol. The day God set me free from alcohol, I was sorry I had ever had a drink in my life. I was so sorry of the times I might have even gotten drunk. I was sorry! I repented with everything that was in me and as a result of genuine repentance, I don't have enough strength in my hand today to lift one ounce of gin, whiskey, vodka, wine or beer, because when you repent unconditionally and completely, there will never be a desire to do anything against God.

The last Greek word is *"ametameletos"* which means irrevocable. In other words, "God, I am turning back. I am turning back. I will never walk that way again, because I have made an irrevocable decision, a decision which cannot be reversed or annulled." You may be *"ametameletos"* and not cry a tear, all you need is true repentance in your heart—godly sorrow.

Scriptures state in Hebrews 4:12 (KJV), *"For the word of God is quick, and powerful, and sharper than any two-edged sword, piercing even to the dividing asunder of soul and spirit, and of the joints and marrow, and is a discerner of the thoughts and intents of the heart."* We may fool ourselves sometimes in our motives or intentions, but God knows our hearts. He knows true repentance, and true repentance will launch you into the overcoming life you have desired.

I am going to ask you to do something special for yourself. When you go to bed tonight, say this prayer and mean it from the uttermost parts of your being:

"Father, I am not just saying a prayer. I am not just saying words. I am saying something from my heart. Lord, I am sorry for

every avenue in my life which is not pleasing to you. I am sorry for those things of the world onto which I am still hanging. From this day forward, because I am repenting in my heart, I will turn around and go in the other direction. I will look to you for strength. I will look to you for power. I will never again look to myself. Forgive me of the things to which I have clung, and Lord Jesus, come into my clean and repentant heart to stay forever. Jesus, please possess me so I can possess your clean and pure mind!"

CHAPTER FIVE

WHAT DOES JESUS SAY ABOUT "FAITH"

Because we possess the mind of Christ we should look upon faith exactly the same way Jesus does. Much has been said in recent years in an attempt to categorize and legalistically define faith. I know we have all heard sermons and sermons and sermons describing faith and I know we ourselves have given many talks on the subject of faith. However, let's take it apart and look at it from the eyes of Jesus and with the mind of Christ.

If I were to make one simple, uncomplicated sentence describing faith, I would say that faith is simply receiving what God has for you. I want you to meditate on that definition and let your mind expand and go into all different directions to see if that doesn't really cover all that faith is. Faith is just having enough trust in God to believe everything He says. If you believe what God says, then you will be able to receive what He has for you.

Faith is not something that can be conjured up, nor can it be emotionalized to a point where it becomes an effective kind of faith. Emotionalism will oftentimes cause us to cross over into the area of presumption rather than allowing our own faith to develop and become strong.

The times in our lives when our faith has been the very strongest has not been a super-hyperventilating time when we were sitting with a group of other believers and begging and pleading with God for more faith. No, the greatest moments of our faith have been in the quiet solitude and constant knowledge and unquestioning belief that God is going to do what He says He will do.

Real faith is never something that is worked up. If you are honestly operating in faith, it will be a solid, constant, abiding calmness, joy, and peace that permeates your very being to such a degree that there is no room at all left in your mind for any doubt or unbelief.

Doubt and unbelief are both the opposite of faith. When we allow questions to come in, such as: "Is this really God's will? Is God going to do it? Am I really going to come out of this situation?", we are allowing doubts to come in which cause us to operate on the negative side of faith.

Jesus spoke very well about this in the eighth chapter of Matthew starting with verse 5 which reads, "*Now when Jesus had entered Capernaum, a centurion came to Him, pleading with Him, saying, 'Lord, my servant is lying at home paralyzed, dreadfully tormented.' And Jesus said to him, 'I will come and heal him.' The centurion answered and said, 'Lord, I am not worthy that you should come under my roof. But only speak a word, and my servant will be healed. For I also am a man under authority, having soldiers under me. And I say to this one, 'Go,' and he goes; and to another, 'Come,' and he comes; and to my servant,'Do this,' and he does it.' When Jesus heard it, He marveled, and said to those who followed, 'Assuredly, I say to you, I have not found such great faith, not even in Israel! And I say to you that many will come from east and west, and sit down with Abraham, Isaac, and Jacob in the kingdom of heaven. But the sons of the kingdom will be cast out into outer darkness. There will be weeping and gnashing of teeth.' Then Jesus said to the centurion, 'Go your way; and as you have believed, so let it be done for you.' And his servant was healed at that same hour."*

Did you notice that Jesus said, *"I have not found such great faith, not even in Israel!"* Jesus was really commenting on this man's faith simply because he did not have to have a show of Jesus. He did not demand and command and say, "Now Jesus, you drop whatever you are doing and come down and you touch my servant." He had so much faith in the ability of God to perform through His Son, Jesus Christ that he very calmly said, "You don't even have to go. You just speak the word and it will be accomplished."

Seek God and faith will come easily.

The outstanding quality exhibited by the centurion is the fact that he had an unwavering, unmixed, undiluted, pure kind of faith. There was no doubt, no unbelief, no questioning, no nothing except simple real faith.

Jesus said to him, *"As you have believed."* That word "believed" covers a multitude of answers and non-answers to prayer because many people have tried to generate faith and have tried to confess faith instead of just receiving and believing what God has for them.

Since we possess the mind of Christ, how do we get our mind into a position where it will be capable of receiving the thoughts of God? Jesus never questioned the mind of His Father. Jesus never questioned the ability of His Father. Jesus never questioned the desire of His Father. He just believed His Father, and was determined to do all His Father sent Him to earth to accomplish. It wasn't simply the fact that the centurion made the statement, but he *believed* what he said. Many times we think we are stepping out in faith, but we don't really believe; we are just hoping that something good is going to happen.

Mark 4:37-41 tells about the great storm that arose when the disciples were in the boat with Jesus. The very first thing they said when the storm came up was, *"Teacher, do You not care that we are perishing?"* Jesus came right back at them and said, *"Why are you so fearful? How is it that you have no faith?"*

Jesus told his disciples very plainly that they didn't have any faith, because they were fearful when the problems came up. The same thing is true of us today. If we actually believe that we possess the mind of Christ, we are not going to be fearful in times of storms, distress or troubles.

Notice that the man with the sick servant had no feelings of panic saying, "You've got to come right now. If you don't, he'll die." He was very calm and said, "Speak a word and my servant will be healed." However, fear, which is the opposite of faith, immediately came into the disciples. Those two circumstances are wonderful examples of what happens when you believe and when you don't.

Let me ask you a question. If you were in a boat with Jesus and a big storm came up, would you be the least bit frightened? Not me, because I know I would be right there with the One who has all power in heaven and on earth.

Jesus had a lot to say about unbelief to His disciples. Matthew 17:14-21 is a good example of this. A man had come to Jesus with an epileptic son and told Jesus that he had brought him to the disciples but they could not cure him. Jesus rebuked the demon and he came out of him, and the child was cured. Then the disciples said, *"Why could we not cast him out?"* Jesus said to them, *"Because of your unbelief."*

Unbelief and faith are two absolute opposites, and Jesus never had any unbelief in His mind, His heart, or His Spirit. But then look at what Jesus said. He didn't say, "If you had great big faith, you could have done it." He simply said, *"If you have faith as a mustard seed, you will say to this mountain, 'Move from here to there,' and it will move; and nothing will be impossible for you."*

Jesus is not saying to us that because we possess

His mind we are going to be possessed of great faith. He simply says, "Have that little bitty kind of faith which has no room for doubt and unbelief."

If we could just begin to believe that it is not trying to manufacture and to weave and to dream up an imaginary kind of faith, but it is simply getting back to little basic principles where we believe everything Jesus said.

To me, one of the most exciting examples in the entire Bible (and I know there are many and each of us has a favorite) where faith is concerned is the story of Shadrach, Meshach, and Abed-Nego.

Think of their simple faith when they replied to Nebuchadnezzar's question, *"But if you do not worship, you shall be cast immediately into the midst of a burning fiery furnace. And who is the God who will deliver you from my hands?"* I love their answer. They said, *"O Nebuchadnezzar, we have no need to answer you in this matter. If that is the case, our God whom we serve is able to deliver us from the burning fiery furnace, and He will deliver us from your hand, O king."* And then look at what they said, *"But if not, let it be known to you, O king, that we do not serve your gods nor will we worship the gold image which you have set up"* (Daniel 3:15-18).

The thing that is so beautiful to me in this particular story is the fact that they were willing to give their life to prove that God is God. Sometimes, to prove that we have "hyper-faith", we get out into an area where we think we are putting God on a spot so He will have to do what we want. Often we are merely showing off a lack of faith.

I remember years ago there was a problem in the state of Mississippi where terrifying riots were going on between the blacks and the whites. A man walked out in front of a bulldozer and said, "God will protect me." But, I have news for you. The bulldozer ran right over him and mashed him "flatter than a flitter" and killed him "deader than dead." He was not operating under the unction of God when he did this, but Shadrach, Meshach and Abed-Nego had a relationship with God which was so firm that they experienced a supernatural miracle. They knew beyond a shadow of a doubt that they were coming out unharmed.

Maybe your faith is like mine. There are times when I have faith for whatever situation is in front of me and then there are times when my faith is not quite that strong. If I began to speak it and say I believed it, I would really in effect be telling a fib. But, if I walk quietly, in my heart believing and trusting God for other things, little by little I have discovered that my faith will grow to the point where I will believe God for the thing I might not have been able to believe Him for one year, two years, three years, or ten years before.

One year when Charles and I were at PTL Club for their annual parade, two separate times God gave me simple faith to know that I heard His voice, and they both resulted in seeing the glory of God.

On Sunday night there had been hundreds of tents all over that great Heritage USA, and it began to thunder and lightning, and the rain came down in buckets. It was like a monsoon. Can you imagine camping out in a tent with rivers of water two feet deep running through your tent?

By the next morning the tents had really disappeared. We had to get up at 5:15 to be at breakfast by six o'clock so they could give us information on the floats. We went downstairs and it was still pouring down rain. It was some of the soggiest weather we had ever seen and was black as night outside.

The staff at PTL put us in vans and took us to the parade site. Even though the rain had slacked up, the skies remained overcast, and it was the gloomiest day you ever saw. We climbed up on our float and it was so wet, the water on the float seeped up on the long dress I was wearing. The entire bottom of my dress for about six to eight inches was soaked in water.

About that time, one of the local television stations came over to ask if they could have an interview with us. They said, "What do you think the chances are for the parade?"

I said, "No *chance* at all." With God there never is an element of chance. I simply said (because God spoke to my heart), "The sun's going to come out and there's not going to be a drop of rain on the parade."

I wish you could have seen the expression on the man's face. I was operating in a supernatural realm of faith, because I had positive knowledge that I had heard God. I was looking at the rain, the overcast sky, and momentarily (in the natural) I thought, "What did I say?" And right on television everyone heard me say, "There isn't going to be any rain on the parade today."

God had given me that supernatural faith He gives to each and every one of us on those very special occasions. About 30 minutes later there was a little tiny blue place in the sky no bigger than a man's hand. With Elijah, it was just the reverse. He saw a cloud the size of a man's hand. There was a little tiny blue spot and Charles nudged me and said, "Honey, take a look at that blue spot up there no bigger than a man's hand."

I said, "Hallelujah! But it's going to grow, and grow, and grow." Not a single drop of rain, not one single one fell on that entire parade.

We ministered after the parade on the PTL satellite, and someone ran up to me and said, "There's a mute here who has never spoken in all her life. She's 28 years old."

I thought, "I'll pray for these short arms over here because that's easier." You see, I have one hundred per cent faith for some things, but when it comes to a mute, I don't always have quite that much faith. Charles and I are always honest, and that's the reason I'm sharing this with you.

I went to pray for the arms and again I heard the small still voice of God. He said, "Is it any harder for me to heal a mute than it is to heal a back or change the weather?" I dropped those arms and thought, "How silly! Isn't it ridiculous that we let the devil come and tell us that we can do the little things, but not the big things?" I said, "Where is that mute?"

God had suddenly poured on me a tremendous gift of faith and I looked at her and thought, "That's no harder than anything else." God's power is always the same. He doesn't make any differentiation where it flows.

This faith that I had heard God was bursting within me and I said, "Stick out your tongue." She stuck out her tongue at me, so I just laid my fingers on her tongue and said, "You dumb spirit, in the name of Jesus, I've got more power than you have, so come out of her right now."

For twenty-eight years she had never said a word in her entire life, and I whispered in her ear, "Say Ma-ma." And she said, "Say Ma-ma!" I was never so shocked in my life because I've never heard a mute yell that loudly when they got healed. She really yelled, and so I said, "Say Pa-pa." And she said, "Say Papa."

Suddenly, it dawned on me that she had never heard her own lips say "Mama" before, so I pointed to her mother, a beautiful gray-haired lady standing nearby whose heart was just broken because her daughter had been mute for twenty-eight years. I pointed to her and said, "Mama."

The girl looked at her mother and said, "Mama!" For the first time in all of her life she could speak the name of the woman who had taken care of her all this time. How I praise God for that supernatural gift of faith that He gave me, and yet it was so simple, because I knew I had heard God speak. I didn't work it up, I didn't get emotional, I just heard God and received what He had for me. Faith is simply receiving what God has for you. Glory!

Jesus healed a deaf mute as recorded in Mark 7:31-37. *"...And they were astonished beyond meas-*

ure, saying, 'He has done all things well. He makes both the deaf to hear and the mute to speak.'"

Doing the same things Jesus did while He was on earth for the glory of God is a twentieth century example of possessing the mind of Christ Jesus! He's alive!

Faith is a growing process. It is not a "jump in and I've got it all" situation. It is a process of development and I believe every problem we face and subsequently overcome is a step in the right direction so our faith will be able to be more like Jesus'!

Recently, in a situation which was acted out in presumption, somebody said to me, "Give me a word of wisdom. Should we continue believing God to supply the money we need or should we go back home?"

I said, "If you have to *ask* me, you are trying to ride on my faith, and you can't do that; you have to operate on your own faith, because when you have to ask somebody, 'should I continue to stand in faith?' that means your faith has wavered and you have lost because you have not continued to believe God."

The thing that is so exciting in the story about Shadrach, Meshach, and Abed-Nego is that their faith never wavered a single solitary bit. They didn't have to question whether or not God was going to do it; they positively knew beyond a shadow of a doubt. But notice that once their decision was made to trust God even to giving their life if necessary, they moved into the seemingly impossible situation with total confidence in God. They never stopped to think, "It doesn't seem to be working!" They walked into the fiery furnace of sudden death in the natural, but they kept walking.

When we are developing our faith by spiritual calisthenics, each step forward strengthens our faith, so when you start into some untested area of faith, keep walking and trusting God!

We have learned also that if God has not spoken clearly enough, we will go to a doctor rather than die standing on what we call faith! God speaks much about common sense along with faith, so we must practice faith daily, practice hearing God daily in our normal day-to-day functions, and then our faith will grow so we can hear God in bigger and bigger needs. After all, faith is a gift and we don't earn it, we just walk in it simply trusting God.

There are times when we say we believe and yet, in our hearts, we know good and well we do not. This has been one of the problems in the great faith movement which was such a big wave for about ten years. As people began to read the Word of God and study the Word of God and stand on the Word of God, it also brought out some immature people who quoted faith, but in their hearts did not believe at all. God has a very secret way of looking within the very depths of our heart to know whether or not we actually believe or whether we are just speaking words. He wants us to trust Him and He is glorified when we do.

I think if we will just try to uncomplicate faith, if we will just try to take out all of the super-hyped faith confessions and get back to a simplicity in faith, we'll be a lot better off.

Charles and I have noticed many, many times that we are forced, because we *are* in a ministry, to make daily decisions which involve faith. We have discovered that what some people think is faith is nothing but stepping out in front of what God really has planned for you at that particular time. Many people have difficulties because they go beyond where God has called them at that specific time.

One of the greatest types of faith you can ever have is faith in the knowledge that you have heard God whether it is for a little thing or a big thing. God may be wanting a little thing in your life at this exact moment of time and yet in the ego trap into which we often fall, we may want a bigger thing than God has planned for us at that moment or for which we are ready. It's really a question of trusting the fact that you are able to hear God in every little nitty gritty area of your life.

Sometimes the choice we make is not a *big* decision requiring a lot of "faith", but it's just the knowledge that we are hearing from God.

We need to listen to God more instead of asking God for more. People can often get involved in programs or projects, which are a desire of the flesh thinking "I would like to have a big ministry. I would like to have a big church building. I would like to have this. I would like to have that," and feeling that it is in accordance with God's will instead of listening for God to tell them what to do. If we let God tell us what to do, then we can always rest assured that we will be successful. If we have to con-

stantly knock on the door of the throne room of God
begging, pleading, crying, and cajoling, we are actually trying to force God to do what we want Him to.
There is a very fine line in the area of faith in this re-
spect and it is so important for us to learn to listen to
those little things of God. It takes just as much faith
to hear God in the little things as it does in the big
things.

So many times people feel that they have heard
God when it is really a thought that comes from
their flesh or from the devil (I don't know which),
saying "God told me I am going to have a big ministry and I'm going to go overseas and I'm going to
speak to hundreds of thousands of people." That
same individual has never led one person on their
block to the Lord. Was that God or flesh speaking? If
we really went back and checked that thought
again, we would discover in all probability it came
from the flesh and not from God. When you come
right down to it, a thought like that is for *your* own
glory rather than for the glory of God.

One of the things we have discovered is that if
you listen to God, the things you accomplish will be
for His glory and not for your glory. That is always a
good test as to whether or not it is you or God. If you
are dead to self, the desire of your heart will be to
please God; if you are not dead to self, the desire of
your heart will be to please self. If we check our motives, it is easy to discover what faith really is and
how simple it is to operate in complete faith at all
times.

"BIG" faith is wanting to please God. Charles

just said that and there is a tremendous truth in that statement.

Why did Jesus have so much faith? Because he wanted to please God.

CHAPTER SIX

WHAT DOES JESUS SAY ABOUT "LOVE"

Because we possess the very mind of Christ, we also possess the very heart cry of Christ.

We possess the very compassion and the very love of Jesus Christ. We possess the same attributes as God because Jesus and His Father are one.

Because we are partakers of the divine nature of God, we have the mind of Christ, the nature of God, the ability of God, the character of God, the wisdom of God, and the love of God.

How should we treat those around us? How should we treat those we love? If we really do have the mind of Christ, how should we treat those we don't love?

Probably one of the best chapters in the Bible about possessing the mind of Christ where love is concerned is in the book of John.

We are surrounded with love. We are filled with love. We are overflowing with love. We are running over with love.

What a privilege, what a joy divine, what a

glorious knowledge to know in our hearts that all these things are ours because we belong to Christ Jesus and because we possess His mind.

The Living Bible beautifully expresses such a promise of God's love. God's love flowing into us enables us to reach out and love those who need love so badly.

"The one who obeys me is the one who loves me; and because he loves me, my Father will love him; and I will too, and I will reveal myself to him"(John 14:21 TLB).

The 23rd verse says, *"Because I will only reveal myself to those who love me and obey me. The Father will love them too, and we will come to them and live with them. Anyone who doesn't obey me doesn't love me."*

What an absolutely mind-boggling statement for us to be aware of. All we have to do is obey God and then both Jesus and the Father will come and live in us. They will love us, love in us and love through us. The world out there that needs so desperately to be loved is going to feel the agape love of God which flows through our veins simply because we are obedient to Christ Jesus.

A long time ago, I heard somebody say that God would not share His glory with anybody. However, if you read the book of John, you will see that we *are* the glory of God. What an absolutely extravagant statement to make. And yet, it comes directly out of the Word of God because we possess the very mind of Christ.

Jesus told us in the 15th chapter of John that He

is the vine, and His Father is the Gardener. And He told us to abide in Him and let Him abide in us.

I love what it says in the 9th verse of that chapter. Jesus says, *"I have loved you even as the Father has loved me. Live within my love. When you obey me you are living in my love, just as I obey my Father, and live in his love. I have told you this so that you will be filled with my joy. Yes, your cup of joy will overflow! I demand that you love each other as much as I love you."*

Do we fully realize what we really have in Jesus Christ? He loves us so much that He wants our cup of joy to be filled. Because I possess the mind of Christ, I am going to be filled with the joy of Jesus all of the time.

Possessing the mind of Christ means agreeing totally, 100% with everything Jesus said. If He says He came that we could be filled with His joy, then I am going to be filled with His joy and my cup of joy is going to absolutely overflow.

What does Jesus say about loving one another? He says, "I *demand*," which also means "I *command* you to love one another as much as I love you. I *require* you to love one another as much as I love you. I *charge* you with responsibility of loving your brother in Christ as much as I love you."

That is the mind of Christ. The desire of Jesus is that we love our brothers and sisters in Christ as much as He loved us.

There are times in the Christian world when brothers begin to criticize and condemn each other. This is the carnal mind which is at enmity with God.

When you criticize a brother in Christ, you are not being obedient to Jesus who commands us to love one another just exactly the way He loves us.

In recent years we have seen many of the large ministries get criticized, and get cracked down on by other Christians. This criticism is the result of operating in a carnal or a fleshly realm instead of operating and possessing the mind of Christ at all times. This same criticism causes strife and division in churches!

If we see a brother doing something we don't like and suddenly feel condemnation towards him, we should *stop* immediately. We ought to go to him in God's love, not in hate. We must continue in a beautiful attitude of love saying "Look brother, your program seems to have a problem. Let's discuss some other options. Let's pray about it." We must act in love just like Jesus did.

The Amplified Bible, John 17:8-10 has some beautiful words on how we should feel because we possess the mind of Christ. *"For the uttered words that You gave Me I have given them. And they have received and accepted [them], and have come to know positively and in reality—to believe with absolute assurance—that I came forth from Your presence. And they have believed and are convinced that You did send Me. I am praying for them. I am not praying (requesting) for the world; but for those You have given Me, for they belong to You. All mine are Yours, and all that are Yours belong to Me; and I am glorified in (through) them—they have done Me honor, in them My glory is achieved."*

Do you realize what He said? Jesus said if we believed with absolute assurance that He came forth from the presence of God then WE ARE HIS GLORY. Possessing the mind of Christ means believing we are the very glory of Jesus Christ Himself!

Isn't that dangerous to know that you are the glory of God? Absolutely not. If anything should make you love the almighty God even more than you love Him right now, it is the knowledge that you *are* the very glory of Jesus Christ!

I love what John says just a little bit further in that same chapter. Verse 16 says, *"They are not of the world, even as I am not of the world"(KJV).* The first time I ever read that verse I nearly exploded. Right along the side of my Bible I wrote, "PTL-Praise the Lord!"

Possessing the mind of Christ means that we do not have to go along with the world.

We do not have to go along with the things the world tells us to do.

We do not have to go along with our peers.

We do not have to dress as everybody else does.

We do not have to acquire the habits everybody else does.

We do not belong to this world any more than Jesus does.

If the world hates you because you do not conform to smoking, drinking, dancing and going to worldly picture shows, all I can say is, "Glory to God. That is certainly a marvelous indication that you possess the very mind of Christ."

The 18th verse gives us even more advice for possessing His mind. Jesus says, *"As thou has sent me into the world, even so have I also sent them into the world" (KJV)*.

If we possess the mind of Christ, then we are going to know we are sent into the world—maybe not the world around us, but our own little individual world which includes our family, our children, our parents, our brothers and sisters. We are sent into *our* world to share the good news about Jesus Christ.

One time a lady called and asked me to pray for her mother who was dying. She was not saved and this lady did not want her mom to go to hell. She said, "Would you pray that God would save her?"

I said, "Have you ever shared Jesus with your mother?"

She replied, "No, I'm afraid to."

"That is part of the commission God gave you," I said. "I want you to hang up this telephone, go to the hospital and share Jesus Christ with your mother right now."

She immediately went to the hospital and shared Jesus with her mother. Her mother died, but she died with Jesus in her heart. Hallelujah! Do you understand what this girl would have missed if she had not possessed the mind of Christ and known that she had a responsibility to go and share Jesus with her mother?

Possessing the mind of Christ is a subject which has no beginning or ending. You can find Jesus in every book in the Bible whether it is the Old Testament or the New Testament. Every thought of Jesus was saturated with and soaked in God's love for people. We will also be saturated with and soaked in the same love for people if we possess the mind of Christ. Think Love! God's love!

CHAPTER SEVEN

WHAT DOES JESUS SAY ABOUT "JOY"

Joy is a priceless and invaluable commodity a-vailable to the Christian. Not something that can be bought or sold, but a gift available to every born-again believer from the Lord Jesus Christ!

My own joy started the day I was saved. I was so completely overwhelmed with thanksgiving when I realized that all my sins were forgiven, that my joy just bubbled up and overflowed. What an explosive thought—my sins were forgiven, ALL OF THEM! I literally wallowed in the glory of that moment for weeks, and then realized that something more had to be done to keep that "up" level going strong all the time!

If we want that eternal spring of joy welling up and bubbling over in us at all times, we need to get into the Word of God for a spiritual feast, take big bites and continue chewing until our souls are fat. The real lasting genuine joy never comes until we are spiritually fat!

Jesus had a lot to say about joy, and since we possess His mind, we need to agree with Him in every area. *"If you keep My commandments, you will abide in My love, just as I have kept My Father's commandments and abide in His love. These things I have spoken to you, that My joy may remain in you, and that your joy may be full"* (John 15:10-11).

This particular portion explains better than any other how Jesus feels about joy. He had to have joy, or He would not have said in the last verse that *"My"* joy may remain in you. He expected that we would have joy and gladness, or He would not have said, "that *your* joy may be full".

Jesus said His joy and delight would remain in us, and our joy would be full, full, FULL! Not just a partial cup of joy, but one that is full measure, complete and overflowing! All of this is ours if we will just stay vitally united with Him at all times. He wants us to have the absolute maximum of joy in our lives at all times. Glory!

Charles and I have often been asked how we maintain the hectic, grueling schedule we keep all the time. Nehemiah 8:10 gives the answer, *"The joy of the Lord is your strength!"* Marilyn Hickey was talking to us recently after we had returned from a super long trip, and she said, "The JOY of the Lord is your total strength, isn't it? You'd never be able to accomplish what you do if you didn't absorb your strength from the joy of the Lord!"

Another friend said about us, "They refuse to let anyone or anything steal their joy." Think about that for a moment. If you allow circumstances or people, or yourself (by thinking about yourself) to take your attention away from God and service to others, you will find yourself becoming discouraged, discontent, depressed, worried, up-tight, or having some other negative selfish attitude come into your heart.

If you want something to sap your strength fast, let that happen to you! But if you want to keep strong and healthy, let the JOY of the Lord be your STRENGTH!

"Jesus realized they wanted to ask him so he said, 'Are you asking yourselves what I mean? The world will greatly rejoice over what is going to happen to me, and you will weep. But your weeping shall suddenly be turned to wonderful joy (when you see me again). It will be the same joy as that of a woman in labor when her child is born—her anguish gives place to rapturous joy and the pain is forgotten'" (John 16:19-21 TLB).

If you're a mother, can you remember when you had your baby? Remember how much it hurt? No, none of us do. We know how painful childbirth can be, and yet when you see that darling little boy or girl God gave you, your anguish gives way to rapturous joy and the pain is forgotten. I will never forget the first thing I said to the doctor after my son Tom was born. His daddy was overseas fighting for the Navy, and I wanted a brown-eyed boy that looked just like his daddy. The nurse had said to me, "Don't scream until the last pain, because remember each one is going to be worse than the one before," so when the last one got there I was waiting for the next one which never came! Then came the good news after all the bad pains. "It's a big boy!"

I said, "My cup runneth over—let me kiss him!"

My cup of joy was overflowing all over the place. I wasn't even a Christian, but in that moment when birth actually took place, I instantly forgot all the pain and all I could think about was how I wanted to kiss that little bundle of humanity God had given me. Just as the Scripture had said, *"her anguish gives place to rapturous joy and the pain is forgotten."*

Jesus says, *"You have sorrow now, but I will see you again and then you will rejoice, and no one can rob you of that joy!"* (John 16:22 TLB). No one can rob you of that joy! Beloved, don't you ever let anybody take that joy out of your life. The devil will do his best to rob you of every bit of your Christian joy, but remember it's Jesus' joy that you have!

Continuing with John 16:23-24. *"And in that day you will ask me nothing. Most assuredly, I say to you, whatever you ask the Father in My name He will give you. Until now you have asked nothing in My name. Ask, and you will receive, that your joy may be full."*

Because we possess the mind of Christ, we need to agree with Him in every single area, and JOY is one area He talked a lot about. Christians should never run around with long faces, but we should be full of the joy of the Lord at all times. Even right now, I pray for such a big cupful of joy for you that you will instantly be bubbling over with the joy of the Lord.

Were you a "sweet" sinner or a "nasty" one? In our family we always say Charles was the "sweet" sinner and I was the "nasty" one, but the end result would have been the same for both of us. Praise God, the "now" result is exactly the same for each of us. We are constantly overflowing with the joy of the Lord. All you have to do to receive joy into your life is to remember when you were born again, your sins were all forgiven and they were buried in the deepest sea, never to be remembered again. If that doesn't make you run over with the joy of the Lord, nothing will! Just to know your sins are gone, gone, GONE is enough to bring joy to the world's most unhappy person.

Jesus wants us to have an everlasting supply of joy and gives us the conditions to have that never-ending supply. In John 15:7 He says, *"If you abide in Me, and My words abide in you, you will ask what you desire, and it shall be done for you."* If you will give some extra consideration to that scripture and meditate upon it, you will discover something that should make you jump for joy. All you have to do is "abide" in Him and then whatever you ask will be done for you. This might seem strange that you can just ask anything and it will be done for you, but we need to remember that when you "abide" in Him or "go into" Him, your desires will be exactly the same as His desires. That's why He gives us so much leeway to "ask what you desire".

The word joy is used 199 times in the Bible, so it didn't just slip in there accidentally. The parable of the talents is an exciting story about Jesus speaking joy into people who were obedient to Him. When the man returned with five additional talents on top of the original five, Jesus spoke words to him that should encourage anyone who is not full of the joy of the Lord. Jesus does want us joyful. *"Well done, good and faithful servant; you were faithful over a few things. I will make you ruler over many things. Enter into the joy of your Lord"* (Matthew 25:21).

Being obedient gives us the privilege of entering into the joy of the Lord. Jesus must have felt this was a great reward for Him to enter into the most delicious of all joys, the joy of the Lord!

"The kingdom of God is not food and drink, but righteousness and peace and joy in the Holy Spirit" (Rom. 14:17). If we're living in the kingdom of God, then we have not only righteousness and peace, but we also have joy, joy, joy in the Holy Spirit!

"Jesus joy" cannot be erased, obliterated, canceled out or blotted out by anyone but ourselves. Jesus wants you to have joy in your heart at all times because the greatest help in the time of problems and tribulations is that everlasting joy which Jesus puts into the hearts of those who love Him and are obedient to Him.

Anyone in a ministry is subject to problems which arise frequently. The single quality that has taken us through everything which has come up is that constant joy in our hearts, indelibly stamped there by the Master Himself, when He gave us salvation. The problems of the world seem dim in comparison to the joy of knowing that Jesus Christ lives in and through you. Look at all the joy expressed in

Psalms 5:11-12:*"But let all those rejoice who put their trust in You;* (Let's rejoice, rejoice, rejoice)
Let them ever shout for joy, (We don't have to be silent, we can even shout and shout and shout!) *because You defend them;*
Let those also who love Your name Be joyful in You. (I love your name, I love your name, I love your name, so I cannot be anything but joyful, Lord!)
For You, O Lord, will bless the righteous; (Thank you Lord, thank you Lord, for blessing me!)
With favor You will surround him as with a shield." Glory to God, we're surrounded with a shield because God's favor is upon us, therefore I've got the joy, joy, joy, joy down in my heart! Glory!

CHAPTER EIGHT

WHAT DOES JESUS SAY ABOUT "THE MASTER-SLAVE RELATIONSHIP"

The word servant comes from the Greek word *"doulos"*, which has a beautiful meaning. A *"doulos"* is a person giving himself wholly to another's will. Mr Webster describes a servant as a "slave", or "a person ardently devoted to another or to a cause or creed." That is exactly the way Jesus wants us to be—totally submissive to His will, giving ourselves completely to Him, utterly laying aside our own lives and desires just to do His will.

Jesus was a servant of God. He became man to be a servant of God. Jesus gave Himself totally to God's will. We need to give ourselves totally to His will also. We should be so committed to the cause of Jesus Christ that it overwhelms us and totally dominates our every thought.

Once we can truly understand the "slave" relationship we have with the Lord Jesus Christ, we will experience more freedom in our lives than we have ever known before.

Paul said a tremendous thing in the second

chapter of Galatians, verse 20. *"I have been crucified with Christ; it is no longer I who live, but Christ lives in me; and the life which I now live in the flesh I live by faith in the Son of God, who loved me and gave Himself for me."*

If we could get that scripture into our hearts, into our minds and into our spirits, we would possess the "servant" mind of Christ. Dying to self is one of the most important principles we will ever learn when we possess the mind of Christ. Jesus had to die to self in order to please His Father and we have to die to self in order to be able to please God and Jesus.

There is a tremendous message to be gained by the Body of Christ in really learning how to think as Jesus thought. In the seventeenth chapter of Luke, verse 6, Jesus talks about having faith as a mustard seed. *"So the Lord said, 'If you have the faith as a mustard seed, you can say to this mulberry tree, "Be pulled up by the roots and be planted in the sea," and it would obey you. And which of you, having a servant plowing or tending sheep, will say to him when he has come in from the field, "Come at once and sit down to eat"? But will he not rather say to him, "Prepare something for my supper, and gird yourself and serve me till I have eaten and drunk, and afterward you will eat and drink"? Does he thank that servant because he did the things that were commanded him? I think not. So likewise you, when you have done all those things which you are commanded, say, "We are unprofitable servants. We have done what was our duty to do."'"*

Jesus is trying to convince us that there is a master-slave relationship between us and God. We rebel against being a slave, and yet the slave is the one who receives the unmerited grace, the unmerited favor and the blessings of God if we are willing to put ourselves in a position of servitude. If we are willing to completely die to our own desires and our own will and want nothing except the will of God, then we will be that perfect servant exactly like Jesus.

My twentieth century translation of what He said is, "Don't come in and order the boss around." The servant does not come in and put his feet under the table and say, "Boss, you serve me."

Some people fall into a real trap believing that we can command God to do many, many things. Jesus is saying to us, "If you'll just be the servant, then God will say to you, 'Well done, thou good and faithful servant.'"

When we can accept that owner-slave relationship and be so committed to God and Jesus that we have no personal desires of our own, we can begin to operate exactly where God wants us to and receive all the blessings God has waiting for us.

Is it really possible for us to totally die to self and deny fleshly desires in today's world with all the outside interference and competition from the things of the devil?

I firmly believe Charles and I are normal Christians. Neither of us have any desire whatsoever to do anything except what God has called us to do. We work 365 days out of every year. You might ask if we

work on Sundays. Yes, if you want to call it work.
We minister 70-80% of the year in meetings around
the world in addition to our regular office responsibilities and writing books. I believe the reason we
have such tremendous joy is because we have
crucified all the desires we had in our lives before
we became totally committed to God.

Charles used to love vacations before we were
married. He would drive thousands of miles every
year sight-seeing, picking up all kinds of souvenirs
and looking for ways to enjoy the things of this
world. There's nothing wrong with that but God has
replaced seeking pleasure with a burning zeal to do
His work. He still lets us see His beautiful creation
while we do His work.

I used to do the same thing. I'd love to go on vacation and see all the sights. I remember riding
down to the bottom of the Grand Canyon on a mule.
When I got back up, my legs were so sore I thought I
wasn't going to be able to walk for a week.

I thought, "Wow, this is really fun."

Since Charles and I made a total commitment of
our lives to God, we have never had a vacation.

People have often asked, "When are you going
to take your vacation?"

We say, "Never." People take a vacation to get
away from everything. I don't want to get away from
anything. The thing that makes me the happiest is
ministering unto the Lord and doing the things He
has called us to do.

Because we are involved in doing the Lord's
work twenty-four hours a day, seven days a week,

we don't need a vacation.

There isn't a vacation you could give us any place in the world that would compare with our having a miracle service. Take a vacation? No, thank you. I want to be doing the things of God every second of my life. That's my first love.

Now you might say, "How do I get to the point when I will feel that same way? I have to get up every morning at 6 o'clock and go to work collecting garbage for the city where I live. This is my income, this is my job. Truthfully, I can't stand my job, but I have to get up and do it. You mean to tell me you don't think I ought to take a vacation?"

Your circumstances are different than ours. You quite possibly do need a vacation to get away from what you are doing in the secular world. During your one or two weeks vacation I would certainly recommend a retreat or convention where you can rest in the Lord and develop spiritually among other believers. There are many fantastic Christian retreats where whole families enjoy the benefits in a Christian atmosphere.

When we worked in our secular jobs, we chose to use our evenings and weekends to win people to Jesus, so even then we didn't need a vacation. New priorities replaced old ones.

Foot washing, if it were practiced today, would make more of us aware of what the servant-master, owner-slave relationship truly is.

In the thirteenth chapter of John we find an extremely fascinating story of Jesus becoming a slave. *"He got up from the supper table, took off his robe, wrapped a towel around his loins, poured water into a basin, and began to wash the disciples' feet and to wipe them with the towel he had around him."*

Peter immediately got indignant and told Jesus that He certainly shouldn't be washing the feet of the disciples. Peter told Jesus he wasn't going to let Him wash his feet, but Jesus said if He did not, then he could not be a "partner" with Him.

Jesus utterly amazed his disciples when He knelt down and washed their feet. At that moment He was the epitome of servanthood!

To me this is the most beautiful of all the ordinances because I had such a unique experience the first time I ever participated in foot washing.

I could not believe anyone in the twentieth century would wash someone else's feet. My pastor merely teased me and said, "Come and see."

I came. I saw, and I experienced something beyond compare where love is concerned.

When you kneel down to wash someone's feet, you become a total slave to that person. The Master completely humbled Himself when He became a servant. If we could only see that in our own lives! If we would be willing to do anything and everything God calls us to do and Jesus tells us in the Word, we would be able to climb to heights beyond our greatest dreams.

Even at this very moment as I sit writing this book, I remember what I felt the first time I ever washed somebody else's feet. I felt God was so close I could have reached up and wrapped my arms around Him. I was so completely enveloped in His love and so totally engulfed in His presence that it was almost equal to an out-of-body experience.

The same love Jesus felt for His disciples flowed through me as I washed the tiny little feet of my pastor's wife.

A foot washing service conducted under proper circumstances in every church or denomination could be one of the greatest things that could ever happen to the Body of Christ. When you wash someone else's feet, you will feel the very servanthood of Jesus as He washed the disciples' feet.

A long time ago I heard a testimony of a very brilliant young Jewish man who had gone around the world seeking the answer to life. He picked up a hitchhiker in Switzerland and was discussing the problems and futility of life when the little old man to whom he had given a ride touched his hand and said, "Men ought to wash other men's feet!" It was said with so much love it was as though his heart had exploded. That simple little statement caused the Jewish young man to accept Jesus.

One year at our Bible School, as I was teaching on the book of John, I shared with the students my experiences in connection with a foot washing ceremony, and the Spirit of God spoke to me and said to have a foot washing service the next day for all the students.

We quickly made all the arrangements and the next morning I told them what we were going to do. Many of the students were unwilling to participate, so we made it very plain that it was a decision on their part because they would not be forced to participate.

We started with singing in two separate circles.
Charles had the men and I ministered to the women.
We sang, "Oh, How I Love Jesus," and other similar
songs. Pretty soon we noticed other students coming
forward to sit in one of the circles. Before we
finished, not only had all the students participated,
they had even gone over into our office and told our
staff what was happening. Many of the staff participated, too! It was a genuine experience of becoming a servant.

"Men ought to wash other men's feet!"

CHAPTER NINE

WHAT DOES JESUS SAY ABOUT "THE ANOINTING"

"The Spirit of the Lord is upon Me,
Because He has anointed Me to preach
the gospel to the poor.
He has sent Me to heal the brokenhearted,
To preach deliverance to the captives
And recovery of sight to the blind,
To set at liberty those who are oppressed,
To preach the acceptable year of the Lord."
(Luke 4:18,19).

I believe with all my heart that the Spirit of the Lord is upon me. There is no doubt in my mind whatsoever. Why? Because I possess the mind of Christ, I am going to do exactly as He did, and I am going to say exactly the same things He said.

When you say and believe that *"The Spirit of the Lord is upon me,"* it will give you your spiritual goose pimples for the day!

The Spirit of the Lord IS upon you. The spirit of the devil isn't upon you, the Spirit of the *Lord* is upon you. That is a mind-boggling statement! It is a difficult thing to understand, but we need to believe it.

One of the most important things you will ever learn in possessing the mind of Christ so you will think exactly like Jesus did is *"He has anointed me to preach the gospel."* You have been *anointed!* Therefore, the same abilities that rested on Him, the same privileges, the same responsibilities, the same power that rested upon Him, rest upon you.

We don't have to go around pleading and begging and crying and saying, "Oh, God, anoint me. Oh, God, anoint me. Oh, God, anoint me. Oh, God, anoint me." You have been anointed, and therefore, you *are* anointed. You don't have to cry and bellow and holler and say, "Oh, I wish I had the same anointing as Frances."

You already have it! The only difference is that Frances uses hers all the time, and not everybody else does. You need to believe that you have been anointed by God and act on it!

Jesus didn't say, "You have been anointed and that anointing stays there for thirty minutes." He said, "You have been anointed permanently." You can stop right here and say out loud, "I have been anointed!"

We believe an anointing will be on those born-again believers who have made a total, absolute commitment of their lives to God and who have died to self. A baptism of fire comes with the death of the old self-nature, then nothing is left of self except dead ashes. That's what happened to sin offerings in the Old Testament. They were burned until only dead ashes were left. When you die totally to self and all you want to do is to pour your whole self into ministering to others, the anointing will always be there. It is the anointing that breaks the yoke.

On first night of all crusades, Charles talks to the ushers and I take charge of setting up the books. Recently, a lady came by and said, "Are you touching those books?"

"Yes, I'm touching the books."

She said, "Aren't you afraid you'll lose the anointing?"

I said, "No, do you know why? I have been anointed to preach the gospel and it is not going to fall off of me because I touch a book!"

A man asked, "Do you dare talk to people before a service?"

"Yes, I dare talk to people before a service."

"Well, don't you lose the anointing?"

"No, I won't lose the anointing because I have been anointed permanently to preach the gospel." The anointing doesn't come and go like the waves of the ocean. You have either been anointed or you haven't been anointed. Could it be possible if you're not so anointed, you're not so saved?

"But as for you, (the sacred appointment, the unction) the anointing which you received from Him, abides (permanently) in you; [so] then you have no need that anyone should instruct you. But just as His anointing teaches you concerning everything, and is true, and is no falsehood, so you must abide—live, never to depart [rooted in Him, knit to Him] just as [His anointing] has taught you [to do]"

(I John 2:27 Amplified).

Why is the anointing permanent? Verse 28 continues, *"And now, little children, abide (live, remain permanently) in Him..."*

I wasn't anointed before I got saved. But I have been anointed now because I am a child of God. I possess the mind of Christ. I am born again, therefore I have been anointed, and the anointing is there at all times.

I like to mingle with people before a meeting. I like to autograph books. I love to talk to the people. I love to touch them. I love to have them touch me and I love to get hugged and I love to hug them back.

At a Full Gospel Businessmen's Fellowship Convention in Atlanta, Georgia, they hadn't opened the doors to the meeting room. There was a lady in a wheelchair in the hall. I didn't wait until I got into the meeting to minister to her. I didn't have to "work up" an anointing, and I wasn't afraid that I didn't have an anointing. I believe the anointing is there at all times to speak a word that needs to be spoken, to lay hands upon the sick and to heal them.

I said, "Wouldn't you rather walk into this meeting than be wheeled in?"

She said, "Yes."

I laid hands on her and said, "In Jesus' name," and out of that wheelchair she came!

Do I lose the anointing when I mingle with people and talk with them before the service? Does it fly out the window if someone gets healed before the service? No, your anointing is with you at all times. All you have to do is believe it and use it!

If you have the anointing of God only upon special occasions, then you will never be able to minister to the world out there when you go into the grocery store, cafeteria, cleaners or other stores to shop. You are anointed at all times if you really believe it, and whatever comes out of your mouth is anointed of God. The words we speak are Spirit and they are life!

"A good man out of the good treasure of his heart brings forth good; and an evil man out of the evil treasure of his heart brings forth evil. For out of the abundance of the heart his mouth speaks" (Luke 6:45).

Because I possess the mind of Christ, I have to believe that what comes out of my mouth is going to be pure and good if my heart is good and my heart is pure. I have to believe what Jesus said because my mind operates in exactly the same channel His does. Jesus makes it so plain to me that when my heart is right, out of my mouth will come good things, things that will bless people, things that will thrill people, things that will inspire people, and not things that will tear people down.

What is stored up in the heart of an upright, honorable, or intrinsically good man will produce that same kind of good.

If I speak evil out of my mouth, it is because there is evil in my heart. If an evil man stores up in his storehouse those things which are depraved, that is exactly what is going to come out of his mouth. So, praise God, we can bring forth out of our mouth those things which are so pleasing, acceptable and delightful to God!

One night while we were eating in a local cafeteria, we were talking about Jesus and about our Video Schools. We were excited because Video Schools are springing up like popcorn all across the nation. Someone who had just watched two three-hour sessions on our video tapes called us earlier that day with a praise report.

One of the individuals who had come to the Video School said, "I like Frances Hunter, but I don't like those books she has written since she started speaking in tongues. But I do love her teaching, so I am going to come and listen to her. However, I am not going to listen when she talks about speaking in tongues and healing and all that stuff." He continued, "I'm a Baptist and I don't believe in that junk because I don't think it's for today."

Did you know you get trapped when you say things like that? He came to school and was going to watch the teaching which had nothing to do with tongues. Suddenly, without any prompting, he lifted his hands up and began to pray in tongues. He got the baptism of the Holy Spirit just watching the Video School. We were not even talking about the baptism, tongues, or the supernatural; but God spoke to his heart.

He got so excited that he continued to pray in tongues. Then he said, "Does anybody here need to be healed?" Remember, he had just said, "Healing is not for today. Speaking in tongues is not for today!" He got up and laid hands on someone else and they were instantly healed! And do you know what else happened to them? They both fell out under the power of God.

That man couldn't believe it, but you see what can happen when people are really receptive to God?

"He has anointed me..."

As we continued talking about our video schools and Jesus and how God can supernaturally do things through video schools, a man came over to us. Now watch what your anointed words, spoken in a public restaurant can do.

He said, "I heard you talking about my Father."

I said, "Really?"

"Yes!"

We said, "You must be talking about God."

He said, "I am. I was fascinated as I sat there and listened to every word you said, because you didn't talk about anything else."

He asked us where we went to church. We asked, "Where do you go to church?"

He said, "I just moved to town and I was looking for a church where the people talk about Jesus!"

Would you believe anointed words could go out over a bowl of spinach? They really did because that man heard them. And so we had an opportunity to witness to him about freedom in Jesus and about what was happening at the City of Light.

I think it's exciting when you sit at a table in a restaurant and realize people can hear everything you are saying and to know that your words are anointed. Next time you go into a restaurant or a cafeteria, just look around and think, "My words are anointed. They're hitting that table, they're hitting that table, they're hitting that table." Just imagine yourself with little anointed sparks flying out of your mouth and hitting the people at tables all around you.

You never really know what can happen when you begin to believe that your words are powerfully anointed. "Wow! I possess the mind of Christ. I have a special anointing because I have the same anointing Jesus had, and so when I speak the Word, whether it's over spinach or cauliflower, roast beef or fish, Mexican food or Chinese food, those are anointed words that can go out and touch somebody."

I believe that I'm anointed. I believe when I speak into a television camera the anointing of God goes right into it. I believe there are going to be people who will watch some of our miracle services on video and when Charles and I raise our hands to lay hands on somebody, people watching the video on television sets are going to fall out under the power of God. I believe it!

And do you know what else I believe? I believe the same thing is going to happen to you if you can just get the simplicity of this truth into your mind. "I have been anointed. I have been anointed. I have been anointed." And the day that you don't feel very anointed is the day you need to say a hundred times, "I'm anointed, I'm anointed, I'm anointed, I'm anointed. I don't feel like it but I'm anointed. I'm anointed. I'm anointed. It doesn't slide off of me when I don't feel good." The anointing of God is there at all times.

Now, I'm going to show you how you'll never forget it. Do you think Jesus has a forgetful mind? No! Whose mind do you possess? Jesus. Are you going to forget that you are anointed? No.

It is a tremendous thing to know that you are anointed. There are times when I have gotten into the car, possibly to go to a local engagement, after I've been involved in work at the office. Proof reading to make sure there are no misspelled words in a new book or a magazine article is not really very spiritual because that is routine, nitty-gritty work.

The first thing I always say when I rush out of the office is, "God, I thank You that even though I don't feel anointed, I am anointed because You said in Your Word I have been anointed."

You have no idea what that will do to you. Did you ever talk to somebody who didn't receive you or your message of Jesus very well? The next time you start to talk and they start getting you riled, say to yourself, "I have been anointed. They don't know it but I have been anointed. The words that come out of my mouth are anointed words." As long as you believe you possess the mind of Christ, every word that comes out of your mouth is anointed. Those anointed words are good for that other person to hear.

"*To set at liberty them that are bruised.*" There are many people in the world today who are bruised. It's our responsibility to know we're so anointed that our anointed words can go out and heal those who have been bruised in one way or another.

Bruised by what the world has done to them.
Bruised by what some friend has said to them.
Bruised by a set of circumstances that in the natural
look impossible, but in the supernatural are absolutely fantastic!

Now, that didn't say "to heal the sick"; it said,
"to heal the broken hearted". Do you really believe
the Word of God coming out of your lips can heal the
broken hearted?

When I was young, every girl had a broken heart
every weekend because boy friends changed girl
friends and went out with somebody else. "Oh, I'm
crushed! I'll never fall in love again." Did you ever
say that? And then you went right out and fell in love
all over again until the next weekend!

That's not the kind of a broken heart I mean.
There are people whose lives have gotten into such a
mess that there is no way in the natural they can get
out of it. We have been sent to heal those brokenhearted people.

Healing the broken hearted does not mean sym-
pathizing with them. Sympathy points to self, caus-
ing people to look inward which is a tool of the devil.
Sympathy will only intensify their grief and sorrow.
We have been sent to mend, to cure, to repair, to re-
store and to ease the pain of the one who is broken
hearted.

We are to preach *"deliverance to the captives"*.
Who needs deliverance? Anyone who is in bondage
needs deliverance. If they are in jail, they need to be
delivered out of jail. If they are in bondage to alcohol, they need to be delivered from alcohol. Many

times when we think about preaching deliverance to the poor, we think about demon-possessed people. There are many people who are bound by alcohol, drugs, dope, cigarettes, illicit sex, depression, guilt, hate and other types of sin. They are bound by an evil force. We need to preach deliverance to them. We need to tell them that Jesus can totally set them free.

People can be in chains to fear. They can be in the most horrible bondage in the world to money. They can be in bondage to money whether they are rich or poor. Poor people are in bondage because they don't have enough money to pay their bills. Sometimes rich people are in bondage to money because money is their god. We often think we are to preach deliverance only to the poor in finances. Sometimes the poor are the richest and the richest are the poorest.

We are to preach deliverance to the poor person, too. To tell him we have been set free from the curse of the law which is sin, death, sickness and poverty. We have been set free! And we can tell that person, "you can be set free from sin, sickness and poverty."

We are to tell the homosexual there is deliverance!

We are to tell the sick there is healing in the name of Jesus!

We are to tell the devil he has to let the oppressed go free in the name of Jesus!

We are to cast out devils!

You might shudder at the idea of casting out devils until you fully realize that your mind is on the same wave length as Jesus. Then you won't shy away. You will look at them with eyes of compassion and anger—compassion for the one who is possessed and anger at the devil who has attacked them!

When you realize the responsibility you have because you possess the mind of Christ, you will want to cast out devils and set people free.

"And to preach the acceptable year of the Lord." You have been anointed to preach the acceptable year of the Lord! What is the acceptable year of the Lord? Right now. Every year is the acceptable year of the Lord!

Some people think the acceptable year is when Jesus comes back, but I believe the acceptable year of the Lord is any time. I'm going to preach that RIGHT NOW is the day of salvation. Not tomorrow, not waiting six months, but today, because I possess the mind of Christ, so I think like Jesus does.

TODAY is the day of salvation!

Say it again: "I'M ANOINTED!"

CHAPTER TEN

WHAT DOES JESUS SAY ABOUT "GOD'S ACCELERATION AND HIS GLORY"

I'm bubbling with excitement over what Jesus is doing today!

I do believe with my heart and soul that we are living in the last days before the return of Jesus. Before long there just aren't going to be any more days, so however long we have left, let's live in the glory of God!

What should we think and believe in these last days?

Jesus believed in the glory of God. We are also going to believe in the glory of God and the miraculous things Jesus is going to do in these last days. We will believe that things spoken about in the Word of God will be, and indeed are, coming to pass right in front of our eyes.

Because we possess the mind of Christ, we are going to agree with what God says in His Word. We're not going to be out in left field or right field all the time arguing about one thing or another. We are going to line up our lives with the Word. The things we say will line up with and be in agreement with what Jesus said all the way throughout the Bible.

We have already discussed the words Jesus said in the New Testament, but God really spoke to my heart to talk to you about the Old Testament.

You may say, "If I possess the mind of Christ, then I have to be in the New Testament because Jesus wasn't born until the New Testament."

Jesus has been here since the very beginning. In fact, He was here before the beginning. Much of what is in the Old Testament is a prophecy of what has come or will come about in the New Testament. Jesus birth in the New Testament fulfilled what was written about Him during the thousands of years covered by the Old Testament.

Let me show you some of the things which are so timely for this particular hour in the history of the world.

Amos says, "'Behold, the days are coming,' says the Lord, 'When the plowman shall overtake the reaper, And the treader of grapes him who sows seed,'" (Amos 9:13).

Beloved, we are in the days of acceleration. I am constantly hearing about acceleration. Not only do I hear about acceleration, but also about the glory of God and the supernatural moving of the Holy Spirit like we've never seen it before.

There is a supernatural revival that's being birthed in the world today. I don't know of anything which will convince people more of the reality of Jesus today on this earth than the supernatural power of God.

God is accelerating everything because there is a lot to do before the Lord Jesus Christ comes back again. To show you what supernatural acceleration means, I chose this particular passage from Amos. It clearly defines what is happening today.

God is saying, "Watch, take a look, see how I'm accelerating things so rapidly you can hardly believe it."

"The plowman shall overtake the reaper."

To understand what God is saying, visualize two separate scenes in your mind to illustrate the acceleration of God in these end times. I want you to visualize the first part that says, *"The plowman shall overtake the reaper."*

Now, when does a farmer plow? He plows after a crop has been harvested. He plows the leftover plants under to prepare the ground for the upcoming crop.

God is saying the plowman is actually going to overtake the reaper because things are going at such a fast pace. Before you have an opportunity to even reap the crop, God is sending the plowman to plow up the ground.

What does that mean?

"The harvest truly is great, but the laborers are few; therefore pray the Lord of the harvest to send out laborers into His harvest" (Luke 10:2). *"Do you not say, 'There are still four months and then comes the harvest'? Behold, I say to you, lift up your eyes and look at the fields, for they are already white for harvest!"* (John 4:35).

God is saying, "Look, get out there and get that

crop in! Get that whole crop in before it's too late! The plowman is going to overtake you! A new crop is coming up!"

That's really fast, isn't it? The plow is coming down the field before you can even get the old crop reaped.

Look at the next verse in Amos. It says, *"and the treader of the grapes is going to overtake him that sows seed."*

These are the days of acceleration, remember, when things happen so fast you almost have to catch your breath to keep up with what God is doing.

Visualize this scene in your spirit. I decide to plant a grape vineyard. Before I ever get that little seed in the ground, UP it comes!

UP comes the stalk. OUT come the leaves. OUT come the little branches. OUT pop the flowers.

The little grapes begin to form. The little grapes get bigger and bigger and bigger. Sour green grapes turn sweet as they ripen. Suddenly, the grapes are picked and put into the winepress. The juice is treaded out before I ever get the little seed in the ground.

Does that give you an idea of what God is doing today?

Yes, God is accelerating everything!

As Spirit-filled believers, we really need to get on the ball. We need to get out in the fields. We need to begin to do all the things God has been telling us to do. We have the mind of Christ. We should be obedient to what He says.

God's Glory

Did Jesus believe in the glory of God? In John 11:39 Jesus was talking to Martha, the sister of Mary and Lazarus.

Lazarus had just died. Martha thought Jesus had fiddle-faddled around getting there. Thinking Jesus had let her brother die and then just lay there all that time, she was really heartbroken.

Jesus spoke to Martha saying, *"Take away the stone."*

Martha replied, *"Lord, by this time there is a stench, for he has been dead four days."*

In the natural, Martha was right. Lazarus probably didn't smell very good by that time. She was totally controlled by her senses.

Let's look at this with the mind of Christ. If we live in the supernatural world, then we ought to be moved only by the supernatural and never by our senses. When you are born again by the Spirit of God, your spirit takes on an eternal characteristic. You actually become a supernatural person in your spirit.

You are still a physical being. You are still walking on this earth, but your spirit becomes supernatural because your spirit has been born again by the Spirit of God.

We are in the world, but we are not of the world. Our spirit lives in the supernatural realm.

If we really believe that, then what are we going to do? We are going to operate and walk and live in the supernatural glory of God at all times. Why? Because we are not the earthly beings we were before we got saved.

Now, I don't want you to get flaky and way out. Don't think "Ohhh, I'm a supernatural being. I can fly from one building to another."

I've got news for you. You can't!

However, you can operate in the supernatural realm where you trust God more than you ever trusted Him in your entire life before. That's living in the supernatural realm and not in the sense realm.

How do we operate and walk and live in the supernatural realm? By utilizing the mind of Christ. He lives within us. He walks where we walk. He talks when we talk. In every situation, stop and ask a simple question, "If Jesus were standing here right now, what would He say? What would He do?"

Since Jesus is living inside of every born again believer, He is living within YOU. Once your spirit catches hold of the fact that He is always there to guide you, you can always DO WHAT HE WOULD DO in every situation. You will live in the supernatural realm in which He is living today.

Let's go back to Martha for a moment. Obviously, she was totally hung up on the natural circumstances.

Jesus said to her, *"Oh, Martha, did I not say to you that if you would believe, you would see the glory of God?"*

The only way you'll ever see the glory of God is to just believe. BELIEVE is such a beautiful word! When you get to the point where you really believe in the glory of God and the supernatural, you will walk closer to God than ever before. You will then walk in the supernatural at all times.

Jesus said, *"Didn't I tell you, IF YOU WOULD BELIEVE?"*

Just *BELIEVE* and you will see the glory of God! I think the desire of every Christian is to see the glory of God and to walk in His presence.

Pastor Buck said in the book ANGELS ON AS-SIGNMENT that God explained holiness to him in an entirely new light.

"Holiness is very similar to the glory of God. It is the outraying of his personality and his presence. Absence of sin is the result of holiness, not holiness itself. Holiness is literally the character and the nature of God. God is holy!"

When you walk in the glory of God, you are walking in the presence and the personality of God. I personally love to walk in the power and in the presence of God, don't you?

Recently, I received a computer printout on the word GLORY. I have gone through my Amplified Bible marking the words GLORY, or GLORIFIED every time I came across them. Every time I open my Bible to that page, I know that the word GLORY is there. If there were several "GLORY's" on the page, I even put a mark at the top of the page. That mark tells me "WOW! This page is a goodie!"

If you want people to see the glory of God, just digest a few choice morsels from these particular pages. Get a concordance and go through your Bible marking the word GLORY each time you find it.

One of the verses I love the most about GLORY is Numbers 14:21, which says, *"But truly, as I live, all the earth shall be filled with the glory of the Lord."*

Can you imagine if the whole world were believers? Can you imagine the glory of God that we would be walking in? God's glory dims when people don't believe. As a matter of fact, unbelievers don't get to see the glory of God, except on very rare occasions.

Can you just imagine if we were walled in with 1,000, or 10,000, or 50,000 real believers? Do you have any idea of the glory of God that would be present? We would be like Moses. We would have to go into the cleft of the rock. God would have to put His hand over us because we couldn't stand to see the full force of His glory.

Charles and I have been so blessed to be able to have seen the glory of God. The first time was probably ten, maybe even twelve years ago. We were in Redding, California in the Civic Center.

I almost missed what happened because I really didn't know what it was. I thought the place was just suddenly getting foggy.

But something in my spirit leaped, and I knew it was the supernatural presence and the power of God. It was just like waves of the ocean had started to rush in over the back of the auditorium.

This particular auditorium is made like a bowl with seats that go up the back, not on the sides. Just like a wave of the sea, a big cloud came crashing over the seats and rolled to the floor level. The waves continued until they covered everyone in that auditorium.

When you see the glory of God, something definitely happens inside of you. When the glory is present and you accept it, miracles happen with a magnitude difficult for the natural man to comprehend.

The glory of God rolled in that day in Redding, California. What an exciting time that was! When the glory of God touches people, they are either going to be changed spiritually or physically. I really believe it's God's will that they are changed both ways.

A bus came in that day from a place called Paradise, California. Of the people on the bus, fifty percent were sick and fifty percent came because they enjoyed attending miracle services. Every sick person, *every single sick person* on that bus without a single exception was healed by the power of God.

When you sit in the glory of God and you openly receive the glory of God, something is going to happen to you. You can't sit in the presence and the glory of God and come out of it exactly the same. I know for a fact that Charles and I have never been the same from that day when the shekinah glory of God rolled in all over that auditorium.

People have said to us, "What did it look like?"

It looked like a golden waterfall or a golden cloud. You could see the light of God in it and yet it had a beautiful golden hue. It was really gorgeous as it actually covered the entire auditorium.

Three little children who were cross-eyed were healed by the power of God.

A lady who had traveled all the way from Boise, Idaho, had been on the bus the entire day and night before. She was in such agony with rheumatoid arthritis that she could hardly walk, talk, or speak. As she sat under the glory of God, she was instantly and totally healed by the power of God without anybody praying for her, without anybody laying hands on her or doing anything. She got up and began to dance. Hallelujah!

Tremendous healings took place that day. Why? Because somebody laid hands on them? No. When you just sit in the glory of God and feel the presence of God encompassing you, a spiritual and physical change will happen on the inside of you. I just love meetings where the glory of God covers every single person, going into all the little cracks, crevices and corners. Everybody gets healed all at one time.

Possible? Oh, yes. I believe these are the days of acceleration in which we are living right now. We are going to see God heal everyone in audiences.

We have been prophesying for ten years that the day is coming when Charles and I will wave our hands over great audiences and they will be instantly healed.

Why is that going to happen? Why will we see the glory of God like that? Because we *believe,* and that same thing is true for you and also, when you *believe.*

If you can just get your spirit man so in tune with the Word of God, you will believe in the anointing of God, you will believe in the glory of God, and you are going to see things you have never seen in your entire life.

I am excited because more and more people are reporting to us that they are seeing angels. Is that because God has more and more angels to send to earth today?

No. Angels don't reproduce themselves. There are no more angels today than there were 2,000 years ago. However, more and more people have gotten into the Word. The more Word you digest into your spirit, the more you will believe in God's supernatural spirit world. We believe God is increasing angel activities on earth as He accelerates final generation preparation for the return of Jesus.

You will believe all the things God said. Because you utilize the mind of Christ, you will see with your supernatural eyes into the supernatural realm of God. In that realm angels are seen as naturally as viewing people with our natural eyes.

Use the mind of Christ that you possess. With your spiritual eyes, see the angels around you and see the work they are doing in the world today. Jesus knows they are all around and thus, you know that angels are protecting you and working with you wherever you go. (See Revelation 19:10).

God stationed an angel with us in Abilene, Texas, in 1978. He explained to us, "That angel is a special warrior angel that I have sent to protect you and Charles from the fiery darts of the devil until Jesus Christ comes back again."

Wherever Charles and I go, we know we are protected by a giant warrior angel. That gives us an extra feeling of security at all times.

Did Jesus believe in the glory of God? Oh, yes, Jesus believed in His Father's glory or He would never have said to Martha, *"If you would just BE-LIEVE, you will see the glory of God."*

That was a promise He was making to Martha. He was telling her that God loved her so much that He was going to let her get a little sample of the glory of God.

God loves us so much that He wants us to see His glory, too.

Oh, Beloved, just BELIEVE and He will open your spiritual eyes to His glorious supernatural world.

We possess the mind of Christ. Are we going to be scoffers— Are we going to be scorners?

Are we going to say, "I don't believe that is what God is doing today. I don't believe God is sending fire into services. I don't believe God is sending His glory cloud."

Well, have I got news for you! If Jesus said it, Jesus believed it and I'm going to believe it, too. I am looking for more and more of the supernatural to be obvious to the believers.

Let me put in a little word of caution right here. The Bible says, *"signs and wonders will follow them that believe."*

Don't run after signs and wonders—let the signs and wonders run after you. Then when they happen, you will enjoy them even more!

God is doing a new thing. There are certain scriptures I am hearing over and over and over again. Does Jesus believe these scriptures? Yes, be-

cause Jesus believes in the fulfillment of everything
that happened in the Old Testament.

Isaiah, the 42nd chapter, the 9th verse says,
*"Behold, the former things have come to pass, and
new things* (brand new ones) *I now declare, Before
they spring forth I tell you of them."*

He said, "Look, don't look back to what I've
done in the past. Oh, that was great, that was great,
but it has already come to pass, so don't look back in
your memories."

Jesus is saying, "Look, come on, let's get on with
it. *New things,* brand new things *I now declare."* He
goes on, *"before they spring forth, I tell you of
them."*

Isaiah 43:19 continues, *"Behold, I will do a new
thing..."* "Look, I'm doing a new thing!"

We have to get our eyes off the old and look to
the new things God is doing today. The principles
never change, but because of the time in which we
are living, God's methods often change as He speeds
things up.

Read how He says it in the Amplified version.
*"Behold, I am doing a new thing; now it springs
forth; do you not perceive and know it, and will you
not give heed to it? I will even make a way in the wil-
derness and rivers in the desert"* (Isaiah 43:19
Amplified).

You can drive on the roads, or ways, in the wil-
derness of Israel and see the giant irrigation canals
that are rivers in the desert. God's timing is right
now to fulfill these prophecies He made long ago.

Every once in a while we can read a scripture

and not really understand it or maybe it just doesn't make a great impression on us. Perhaps it is not God's perfect timing for us to really understand it at that particular moment.

I always get excited about that particular part of Amos, showing the acceleration to come. I had passed over that verse for years and years and never noticed it!

Amos 3:7, *"Surely the Lord God does nothing, unless He reveals His secret to His servants the prophets."*

I discarded that verse, because I thought, "I'm not a prophet, thus God won't reveal anything to me. The prophets were just in the Old Testament. We don't even have prophets today."

But when God is talking about the five-fold ministry in the New Testament, a prophet is included. A prophet is for today. A prophet is part of the planned ministry for you and me. God does speak to His children and through His children. He reveals what is to come.

A revelation was given to Steve Lightle a few years ago concerning the second exodus of the Jews coming out of Russia. When we heard what God is doing with His chosen people, the excitement and anticipation exploded within us. We know that we are going to see the glory of God where the Jews are concerned.

God spoke through His prophet unto all His children so they could prepare for and rejoice at the victory soon to be manifested during the second exodus of the Jewish people. ALL His children means you and me because we have a special part to play in the living drama soon to unfold.

Let me briefly share the story with you—a real live example of utilizing or possessing the mind of Christ which also illustrates how God is accelerating His activities today to fulfill His prophecies as foretold thousands of years ago.

The publishing of EXODUS II is one of the most exciting in the history of our ministry. EXODUS II shares the vision God gave Steve Lightle, His modern day prophet, of the Jews coming from the North (Soviet Russia) to return to Israel.

The manuscript was brought from Europe and placed in our hands in July. To have it edited, proofread, and at the typesetters within one week was a supernatural miracle of God.

In the natural there was no way everything could have been accomplished. Charles and I operated totally in the supernatural. We believed God could quickly accomplish what it would normally take us five months to do. And that's exactly what God did.

We were not moved by the things we saw.

The world said, "You cannot get a book typeset that fast."

The world said, "You cannot get a book published within thirty days after first seeing the manuscript."

The world said, "You can't do this, you can't do that. These are the laws of the business world."

The world said, "Impossible."

With God however, ALL things are possible.

We were actually working through normal channels to get things done. However, at the same time we allowed God to do His supernatural scheduling.

Many people think, "Ohhh, I'm a supernatural creature. I'm going to operate in the supernatural. I believe in the glory of God. Everything is going to be great."

Then they fail to do what is necessary in the natural to allow God to work for us.

We didn't ask God to send us an angel to typeset the manuscript. We don't believe that is the way God works. God still functions according to the principles down here on earth.

We didn't ask God to take the manuscript up to heaven and print it on an angelic printing press. I doubt very much that there are angelic printing presses in heaven.

However, we did ask God to give us such favor with man that we could go right through all of the little hangups that normally inhibit progress. God saw to it that everything was done according to schedule.

EXODUS II had to be completed and ready to take to Israel for the Feast of the Tabernacles which celebrates the first exodus of the Jews out of Egypt.

We trusted God and did not look in the natural. If we had, we would have agreed that it couldn't be done. But we didn't look in the natural. We know that we don't live in the natural. We live in the supernatural power of God.

God totally put the whole thing together.

EXODUS II was at the feast of the Tabernacles just a few short weeks from the time we were first handed the manuscript in July.

Impossible, you say? No, with God ALL things are possible. And you will believe the same things can and will happen in your life if you learn to utilize the mind of Christ which is within you right now. God told us what to do and then gave us the tools necessary to perform that which He told us to do. He is always so faithful!

God says in His Word, "I'm not going to do anything unless I tell you through your prophets."

Don't miss seeing the glory of God! Listen to what God is speaking forth today through His servants, the prophets.

Read EXODUS II. You'll get excited, too!

Do you think Jesus Christ missed anything? No, Jesus stayed right there in the middle of everything. If you and I are going to be thinking and acting like Jesus, then we're going to be talking like Jesus. We're going to be in on all the things God is doing today.

The Vision of Jesus

At Campmeeting '83 which was entitled "A SUPERNATURAL SPREE", we were worshipping God on a Saturday afternoon. During praise and worship is when you are likely to really see the supernatural power of God.

Directly in back of me appeared a huge white cloud. It was so thick it looked like it actually had substance. I felt as though I could reach out, touch it and get a handful. It was so white it looked like Marshmallow Creme.

I thought "WOW, that's really neat up there, isn't it?"

I did not yet have any idea what was going to happen on this stage directly in back of me. This cloud mushroomed just exactly the way a thunderhead looks in the sky. They always are so super white with that mushroom shape on top. This cloud was also super white and it was mammoth.

As I watched, I thought, "Ohhh, the glory of God!"

My spirit was stirred. You don't have to be judged by whether or not you shake, vibrate or get goose pimples that are ten feet high. People experience the presence of God in different ways.

The presence of God entered the auditorium in a new and different way than I had never seen before. I watched. If I were asked to describe what the cloud looked like up there, I would have to say it looked like a cocoon.

Out of the center appeared the Lord Jesus Christ in all of His glory and His power and His majesty. My heart felt like it literally exploded within me.

Once before Jesus appeared to me in person. We were in a meeting in a little town called Alexandria, Indiana several years ago.

As Jesus sat down beside me, He said, "The anointing is on Charles tonight and he is to speak. You are to listen."

When Jesus appears to you in person, it affects your whole life. You will have an anchor point in your life like never before. You will never again doubt the reality of God. You will never again doubt the call of God.

Jesus appears as a blessing from God and usually as a tremendous surprise. Don't believe that you can ever imagine that Jesus is right here, and thus, see Him. It won't do you a bit of good.

I was so overcome with the presence of God, I just stood there like I had been struck dumb and stared at Jesus as He appeared on the stage just a few feet away from me. All I knew was that I was basking in the glory of God.

Then Jesus went back into the cloud.

"Oh, Jesus," I wanted to cry out. "Don't go away! Don't go away! Come back! Come back! Come back!"

However, I remained silent because the service was still going on.

I was thinking, "How many other people are seeing exactly the same thing I'm seeing?"

I wanted everybody to see Him.

Suddenly, He appeared again.

Excitement coursed through me again. How long he stayed visible I really don't know. When you are seeing in the Spirit, time tends to stand still. What seemed like 12 or 15 minutes could actually have been a matter of a few seconds. I certainly didn't think about looking at my watch. I didn't think about looking at anything.

All I was thinking about was Jesus. I was totally

caught up into the glory of God. Coming and going in and out of the cloud, He appeared several times.

Suddenly, God spoke, "That's the way I want you to be. I want you to be so lost in Him that when people see you, all they will see is the glory of God. All they will see is My glory."

Many times since that day, I have pondered why God allowed such a supernatural manifestation of His presence. The reality of what God was saying came to me very vividly.

"Jesus spoke these words, lifted up His eyes to heaven, and said: 'Father, the hour has come. Glorify Your Son, that Your Son also may glorify You, as You have given Him authority over all flesh, that He should give eternal life to as many as You have given Him. And this is eternal life, that they may know You, the only true God, and Jesus Christ whom You have sent."

He went on, *"I have glorified You on the earth. I have finished the work which You have given Me to do. And now, O Father, glorify Me together with Yourself, with the glory which I had with You before the world was."*

He was saying, Father, while I was down here on the earth I was walking with all that glory. Now, my work is finished. Glorify me together with Yourself with all the glory that I had with You before the world began. Father, do this so they will know You!

"I have manifested Your name to the men whom You have given Me out of the world. They were Yours, You gave them to Me, and they have kept Your word. Now, they have known that all things

which You have given Me are from You. For I have given to them the words which You have given Me; and they have received them, and have known surely that I came forth from You; and they have believed that You sent me."(Extracts from John, chapter 17:1-26.)

Jesus was praying. He was saying, *Oh, Father, I pray for those you have given Me. I don't pray that you will take them out of the world, but that you will protect them from the evil one. I'm praying for those you have given Me for they belong to You. I want them to be in heaven with You and Me, and I want them to see My glory which You have given Me, because they are My glory.*

"And the glory which You gave Me I have given them, that they may be one just as We are one: I in them, and You in Me; that they may be made perfect in one, and that the world may know that You have sent Me, and have loved them as You have loved Me."

Do you understand what He said? Jesus is glorified in YOU and in ME. The Living Bible says, *"And you are My glory."*

Think back to what I shared about Campmeeting. Do you remember what God said?

He said, "I want you to be so in Him, I want you to abide so in Him, that when people look at you they will not be able to see you in the flesh. All they will be able to see is My glory."

When God gives you a revelation you're going to have to sit down and think about it. You're going to have to get back in the Word of God and say, "God, show me in the Bible the message you were trying to give me that day when Jesus appeared."

I began to go back over this seventeenth chapter of John. It became so real to me that God not only wants us to be so abiding in Him, so "going into Him" that when people look at us, when they look at you, when they look at me, all they're going to be able to see is the Lord Jesus Christ.

He is the glory of God so what are they going to see when they look at you and me?

They are going to see only the glory of God.

They are going to see the presence of God surrounding you.

They are going to see an area of holiness around you like they have never seen before.

Do you know what this is going to do to the sinner in this end time? These are the times when God was speaking about when He said, "Put in the sickle. Just put in the sickle."

The fields are so white unto harvest, you don't have to spend time talking to people for hours about Jesus. let the glory of God be so seen upon you that your presence, your very presence will convict the sinner.

At a Christian Booksellers' Convention, we had many opportunities to share Jesus. One morning I had missed the shuttle bus which was taking us down to the Convention Center ten long blocks away. The heat was so intense that I wasn't about to walk.

Having missed the shuttle, I thought, "Well, I'll take a cab."

I started to go out on the same side where the shuttle bus stopped, but there was a little thing in my spirit that said, "No, don't take one of those cabs. Walk through the lobby of the hotel and go out the front. Take the cab waiting there."

As we follow after the Holy Spirit and as we are aware of the glory of God, we're going to become more and more sensitive to little nudges from the Holy Spirit.

Believing that I had heard from the Holy Spirit, I turned right around from where the cabs were lined up, walked out through the lobby to the front of the building and took a cab. The first thing I said to the driver was, "How are you?"

He said, "Terrible."

I said, "What's the matter?"

He said, "I've got no peace, and I can't pay my bills. I'm just miserable!"

Hallelujah, what an opportunity to share Jesus! Now, I knew why God had given me the little nudge and said, "Don't go out that way. Go out the front. I have something for you!"

I replied, "I know the person who has the answer! God loves you. God wants you to be happy and Jesus wants to give you a peace that the world cannot understand. Not only that, He wants you to be happy in every way and to have prosperity and be able to pay all of your bills."

Somewhat surprised the man asked, "He does?"

I said, "Have you ever made Jesus the Savior of your soul and the Lord of your life?"

He answered, "No."

I said, "Would you like to?"

Quickly, he said, "Yes!"

I said, "Pray this prayer."

The cabby prayed the sinner's prayer asking Jesus to come into his heart and asking God to forgive all of his sins. At the end I prayed for prosperity for him and that his soul would overflow with a supernatural peace that would encompass his entire family and their problems. The cab fare was $1.75. I had a five dollar bill in my pocketbook. God said, "Give him the whole five dollars to show him that prosperity is on the way."

As I gave him the five dollar bill, I said, "You just keep the rest of it as a tip."

He burst into tears!

Did I say anything that was very sad? No. It was the glory of God that he saw. I said, "That's God's first step in bringing prosperity into your life."

He saw the glory of God, and he began to become a believer himself. He let God's spirit touch him and move upon him. He wept all over the place.

God has so much to offer if we just realize that all He wants is a total commitment. No person with a sin-stained life is ever going to see the glory of God. God is looking for a people who are willing to make a total commitment of their life to love Him with their mind, their heart, their body and their soul. he is looking for a people who are not interested in the things of the world, but only the things of God.

He's saying, "Get the sin out of your life, get anything out of your life that keeps you from being a part of Me." Does Jesus believe that? Yes! Jesus is coming back for a bride without a single spot or wrinkle or blemish, and these are the days when God is speaking to the Body of Christ about really cleaning up their acts.

I see people who have been hanging onto the little fringe areas, "I still go to movies. I still like to watch television. I still spend all my time doing this."

God is saying to the Body of Christ, "Are you spending all the time you ought to in intercessory prayer? Are you spending all the time you should in reading my Word? Are you spending all the time you should in communicating with me? Are you spending all the time you should winning people to Jesus? He says when you get yourself on that level, that's when He will be able to show you His glory.

Jesus said, *"Make them pure and holy through teaching them your words of truth. As you sent me into the world, I am sending them into the world, and I consecrate myself to meet their need for growth in truth and holiness"* (John 17:17-19 TLB).

Jesus committed His life to meet our need for growth not only in truth, but also in holiness. Let us never let Him down.

Then He said, *"I am not praying for these alone but also for the future believers who will come to me because of the testimony of these. My prayer for all of them is that they will be of one heart and mind, just as you and I are, Father—that just as you are in me and I am in you, so they will be in us, and the world will believe you sent me"* (John 17:20,21

TLB).

Do you remember what I said that God told me? He said, "I want you to be so *in* Him, I want you to be one with Him, I want you to be so *in* Jesus that when people look at you, all they will be able to think about is the Lord Jesus Christ, and the power of conviction will fall over them."

I can hardly wait until the day when God's saints just march down the street and sinners fall down and cry out, "God, save Me!"

Do you think that is far fetched? No, that is not, because that is exactly what God is doing in these end times. You are going to see more and more Christians walking in the glory of God with the joy of the Lord all over them. You are going to be able to see them shining in His glory. You will be able to pick them out of a crowd of a thousand people.

Jesus has separated us and set us apart from the things of the world, and what the world is enjoying. If we get into the Word of God, love God, believe God, and commit our lives to Him, we won't be interested in doing any of the carnal things of the world.

He closes that wonderful chapter in John with some glorious, inspiring promises to you and to me in the twentieth century. *"I have given them the glory you gave me—the glorious unity of being one, as we are—I in them and you in me, all being perfected into one—so that the world will know you sent me and will understand that you love them as much as you love me. Father, I want them with me— these you've given me—so that they can see my glory. You gave me the glory because you loved me before the world began! O righteous Father, the world doesn't know you, but I do; and these disciples know you sent me. And I have revealed you to them, and will keep on revealing you so that the mighty love you have for me may be in them, and I in them"* (John 17:25,26 TLB).

We possess the mind of Christ.

We think the thoughts of Jesus.

We say the words Jesus said. He said the glory God had given Him, He gave to us. Let us walk in the presence of God because we have the mind of Christ.

He's coming back for a bride without a single spot or wrinkle or blemish, so let's be excited about being a part of that bride and walk in the glory of God!

As for me and my house, we're going to walk in the glory of God all the days of our life. Join us!

CHAPTER ELEVEN

WHAT DOES JESUS SAY ABOUT "GLORY AND THE MOVE OF GOD"

At a recent meeting in Decatur, Illinois, on the final night of a convention, the glory cloud of God filled the entire place like a thin cloud of smoke, angels were more numerous than people, and a solid blanket of blue flame covered the entire audience.

Then God spoke, "Which is the hottest, the yellow flame, the orange flame or the blue flame? The blue flame. Therefore I have sent my hottest fire to burn out the sin in your life because I have called this group to a special ministry."

A second word from the Lord immediately followed which concerned getting sin out of lives and receiving a real baptism with fire.

Reports came to us later that we were the only ones who slept that night. The entire 1,500 people who were present were so aware of the glory of God that they could only praise and worship Him who had sent it all night long! It's just as Jesus said, If you will only *believe,* you will see the glory of God!

David said his heart cried out for God. He was

so excited when he saw the Ark of the Covenant coming back that he had to dance before the Lord. He said, *"I am willing to act like a fool in order to show my joy in the Lord"* (II Samuel 6:21 TLB). He said this because the Ark of the Covenant contained the glory of God; David was a man after God's own heart, and he wanted to see the glory of God at all times. So do I!

I have a feeling that the New Testament church was one of the most exciting churches in the world. They certainly didn't sit there like bumps on a log. I believe that every time they got together they had a fantastic, whing-ding time.

I believe they worshipped God. I believe they sang, clapped their hands and jumped around rejoicing because they were in the kingdom of God. I also believe that if you went to church and said, "I've got a pain," that every hand in the church would be on top of your head in nothing flat and everyone would be asking God for a miracle. That's why the Bible records so many miracles which happened when the disciples just walked by and their shadow fell upon people, or when they touched the sick and they were instantly healed, all because the glory of God was there.

Along about the beginning of the 20th Century there was a tremendous wave of the Spirit of God as God mightily poured out His Spirit. People at that time worshipped God with their hands up in the air. "Praise God, praise God, Hallelujah!" They really had fun in church because they believed that church was the most exciting place in the world. But what happens to a lot of people? We get formal after we have gone to church for a while. Did you ever take a look at new converts? They absolutely act like they don't have a bit of sense in their head. They want to run around and tell everybody about Jesus. I remember in my own life, I practically beat people over the head when I first got saved because I had to share with everyone what a man named Jesus had done in my life. I was about as wild as you could get.

The same thing happens when you receive the baptism with the Holy Spirit. You pray in tongues all night long. You get so excited you can't go to sleep and you think the fervor will never wear off and hope it doesn't.

The peculiar thing is, the same things happens in your love affair with God as happens to many married couples. They are madly in love with each other when they get married and can't stand to be apart, but before long they can't stand to be together.

Your love affair with God and your love affair with your husband or wife are alike in many ways. Both of them need to be nurtured. You need to spend a lot of time and attention with each relationship if you want to get the most out of each one. Many times after people have been married for several years, they don't sit nearly as close to each other. They don't hold hands the way they used to hold hands. They don't put their arms around each other. Suddenly, love gets a little bit cooler and a little bit cooler and a little bit cooler. What happened to the glory of marriage?

It should never be that way. You should love each other more, not less. Every day that you are married, every single solitary day that you are married you ought to love God and your spouse more than you did the day before. Marriage is the most exciting institution God ever invented. God laid down the guidelines for it. It's exciting because He wants us to be happy. God does not want us to be unhappy, but it is when we don't do our part, don't nurture, protect, water, and fertilize our love, that love begins to wither and die.

We have been married over fourteen years, and I love my husband in a much wilder way than I did when we were first married. Why? Because each of us does everything we can to please the other one and to make each other happy. That is why our love continues to grow. I'll give you the secret of our marriage. Jesus is the center of our home, the center of our marriage, and the center of each of our lives. I believe that is the only thing that will keep your marriage relationship as exciting as it should be.

Many people do exactly the same thing with God. They get saved, "Glory to God, Hallelujah, I'm saved, I'm saved, and all my sins have been forgiven and forgotten, praise God praise God!" They begin to walk in the glory of God for a while, and slowly something happens. They get involved in the things of the world.

That old song which says, "Turn your eyes upon Jesus, look full in His wonderful face, and the things of this world will grow strangely dim, in the light of His glory and grace," is certainly a good song about the glory of God. People don't always continue to look in the face of Jesus, so the things of this world grow strangely *bright*. As they begin looking in the face of the devil, the things of the world become far more important than the things of God.

Suddenly, their love affair with God and Jesus, which burned so brightly and caused them to walk in the glory of God, has grown lukewarm. There is nothing in the world more disheartening than a love affair that is lukewarm or a relationship with Jesus Christ that is lukewarm.

The ultimate glory of God is never visible until the flame is turned up all the way. I have often said if I were ever going to be lukewarm I'd rather be a wild sinner because the most miserable person in the world is one who knows God, but has walked away from His truth and His glory.

At a meeting in Saskatoon, Saskatchewan, Canada, God did a supernatural miracle to show His glory. People were slain by the power of God by the hundreds. God did it supernaturally because the ones standing in the back of the line fell backwards under the power first, then the next ones until the whole section fell as though a giant vacuum had sucked them down from the back of the line so no one could think they were just a bunch of dominoes that were tumbling against each other. The glory of the Lord had filled the temple!

There was an 84 year-old lady present who was exhuberant with holy laughter. She could not get up off of the floor. Every time she would try to stand up she would fall down again. She said to me, "You know, in about 1905 or 1906 when this great revival started, I saw the glory of God. I saw the glory of God in all church services, but I have never seen it from that day to this." She really rolled her eyes on that statement, then she added, "The glory of God has filled this temple tonight."

The pastor of this great church said, "I've been in Pentecost all of my life and I have never seen anything like I saw happen tonight."

"Arise, shine; for thy light is come, and the glory of the Lord is risen upon thee. For, behold, the darkness shall cover the earth, and gross darkness the people: but the Lord shall arise upon thee, and his glory shall be seen upon thee" (Isaiah 60:2 KJV). That means the glory of the Lord is going to be seen on you. These are the days when we are to walk in the glory of God.

Why was the glory seen so much in the turn of the century? I believe it was because those people were hungry, hungry, hungry for the glory of God. When we become that hungry again, we will begin to walk once more where Jesus wants us to walk—in the glory of God!

"But we all, with open face beholding as in a glass the glory of the Lord, are changed into the same image from glory to glory, even as by the Spirit of the Lord" (II Corinthians 3:18 KJV). That's the way we ought to live at all times, from glory to glory. There's no reason for valleys. We ought to go from glory to glory.

Moses was out herding sheep when suddenly a bush started burning but it wasn't consumed. He saw the glory of God as God spoke to him telling him to quit herding sheep and start herding people. That was the call of God upon Moses' life—the leading of the children of Israel out of captivity. Actually, that depicted Jesus leading people out of sin. The glory of God will still draw people out of their sins.

What is the glory of God? What mystery can it be? How can you know the glory of God? When is it going to come? How is it going to fit into your life? How are you going to fit into the glory of God? Can you see it? Can you hear it? Is it like a rushing mighty wind? Is it like a burning bush? What is it like? How can you behold it? How can we in the twentieth century know the glory of God like Moses did?

Saul of Tarsus had persecuted the Christians, even killing many of them. Even though he thought he was a friend of God, Saul was an arch enemy of Jesus. When he met Jesus Christ personally, the glory of God shining out from Jesus was so overwhelming that Saul fell backwards under the power of God. The glory of God was too much for him to behold. He fell backwards! As a result of that, Saul of Tarsus got saved and baptized with the Holy Spirit. He was blinded! He was healed! He spoke in tongues. Then he went out and preached the gospel and wrote more of the New Testament than anyone else, because the glory of God had touched his life!

Oh, that God would knock a few more Sauls of Tarsus off of their high horses and let them see the glory of God so they would sweep across this nation, across the world, changing lives for Jesus because they had seen the glory of God!

This is the day in which God is displaying His glory mightily, so more than ever we need to believe that God is a supernatural God. Jesus is supernatural. Everything about the two of them is supernatural. We need to believe in the supernatural so we can see the glory of God. I want to see the power and the majesty and the glory of God every day of my life. I want to see the manifestations of God's power. I want to see cripples healed. I want to see children who were born with parts of their little bodies missing totally healed by the power of God. I want to see the glory of God.

What is the glory of God? It can be many things to many different people. To me, the glory of God is the presence of God in everyday living, Jesus walking inside of us and Jesus doing through us the same things He did when He was on the earth. The word of God being fulfilled within the life of every believer is the manifested glory of God!

Did it ever dawn on you that Jesus Christ living in your heart is really the glory of God? I want you to walk down the street and just quietly say to yourself, "Jesus is living in here. Jesus is living in here. Jesus is living in here."

Every time you put your foot down, say, "That's the footprint of Jesus. That's the footprint of Jesus. That's the footprint of Jesus."

When you stretch your hand forth to help someone or lay hands on them for healing, say, "These are the hands of Jesus. these are the hands of Jesus. These are the hands of Jesus."

When you begin to speak it aloud and begin to

believe it with your mind, your soul and every beat of your heart, you will be walking in the glory of God.

I want to see the latter rain. I want to see the former rain. I want to see them both come together which is what is happening today as God accelerates His final thrust before Jesus returns. I want to see the glory cloud of God in services when believers gather together and the glory cloud just fills the place with the presence of God.

I want to see angels. I want to see angels ministering and helping people as we go along in our day-by-day work. That's the glory of God.

I want to see hundreds, I want to see thousands, I want to see millions of people saved. That's the glory of God.

We will never see it if we don't believe. If we will just believe, the glory of God will pour out upon us will be amazing. There's an old song we sang at one of our Campmeetings called, "I'M UNDER THE SPOUT WHERE THE GLORY COMES OUT". That is where I want to sit all the time. That is where I want to be. And do you know why I want to be there? Because that is where Jesus sat.

Jesus sat under the glory spout of God and even though He went to the cross for you and me, He went in the glory of God. Because of the tremendous sacrifice God made and Jesus willingly fulfilled, you and I can walk in the power and the glory and the majesty of God today!

THINK GLORY! JESUS DOES.

CHAPTER TWELVE

WHAT DOES JESUS SAY ABOUT "MISCELLANEOUS CAPSULES:" Prayer, Treasures, Seeking Him First

Almost every "red" verse in the New Testament (words spoken by Jesus) gives us some special insight into how we should think, but there isn't room in a single book to expand on all of them, so I have taken a few on various subjects which can help make your thinking patterns begin to flow in the same manner as Jesus'.

Prayer

Jesus spent a lot of time on the earth praying. There were times when He would pray day and night. Therefore, if we have the mind of Christ, we are going to also spend a lot of time in prayer, which in reality is just talking to God and listening to Him.

Charles and I pray constantly, every waking moment. Someone once said to us, "I'm sure you have callouses on your knees from praying." They were surprised by our answer because we very rarely pray on our knees. We pray ALL THE TIME, and it would be difficult to get our work done if we were on our knees all the time. it would be impossible to write a book on your knees, so we need to learn that praying is a twenty-four hour a day activity or at least every waking moment, and not something that has to be done on your knees.

Prayer is communication with God however you do it. All our thoughts are filtered through God and we talk to Him (think to Him) all day long, in all of our business details, in all of our planning for our crusades, in all of our travel arrangements, in all the books we write and in all the letters we write. Prayer should be such a natural thing that we do it all the time.

There will be special times when you want to do nothing but pray, and draw yourself aside for that purpose, but for the most part, we find the greatest effective prayer life involves an "on-line" communication with God all the time. We never take our thoughts off of God, regardless of what we are doing!

I learned something especially interesting recently concerning the scripture in Matthew 18:19-20. *"Again I tell you, if two of you on earth agree (harmonize together, together make a symphony) about—anything and everything—whatever they shall ask, it will come to pass and be done for them by My Father in heaven. For wherever two or three are gathered (drawn together as My followers) in (into) My name, there I AM in the midst of them"* (Amplified).

We need to learn to "agree" in prayer. What happens if two people are not completely agreed in prayer? Think about with whom you might be a-greeing. Are your beliefs in total agreement, or are you agreeing in certain areas only? We might be in agreement on a certain prayer answer, and yet to-tally disagree in other scriptural areas. We need to get all of our disagreements ironed out before we begin to agree in prayer. Jesus said where two or three were drawn together as His followers (or be-lievers) He would be right there.

Maybe we won't always get prayers answered because we have failed to realize that in possessing the mind of Christ we need to know and believe that when we gather two or three people together to pray, we need to gather two or three people who are "all the way" believers of the Lord Jesus. When there is disagreement in any area of God's Word, this means you are not in agreement. Let's choose as prayer partners those with thom our spirits blend and our beliefs blend, then watch for those answers!

You might say, "What if you pray outside the will of God?" Can you really pray outside of the will of God if you are totally connected to the Lord Jesus Christ? If we are operating with His mind at all times, our desires are not going to be outside of what Jesus Himself would pray. We want what He wants!

"For assuredly, I say to you, whoever says to this mountain, 'Be removed and be cast into the sea,' and does not doubt in his heart, but believes that those things he says will come to pass, he will have whatever he says. Therefore I say to you, whatever things you ask when you pray, believe that you receive them, and you will have them" (Mark 11:23-24).

Because we have the mind of Christ, we are not going to let doubt and unbelief come into our mind. Doubt and unbelief are strictly from the devil and since we possess the very mind of Christ, there is no room for devil thoughts. We're going to pray exactly like Jesus did, we're going to believe exactly the way Jesus did, we're going to expect the same answers to our prayers that Jesus did, and we are going to rejoice because we know the answer is on the way.

Jesus puts a very interesting condition on the end of those scriptures concerning prayer. He gives the secret as to why many prayers are not answered. Verse 25 says, *"And whenever you stand praying, if you have anything against anyone, forgive him, that your Father in heaven may also forgive you your trespasses. But if you do not forgive, neither will your Father in heaven forgive your trespasses."*

Because we are so blessed to possess the very mind of Christ, what are we going to do about forgiveness? If you have been wondering why prayers have not been answered, this is the time to search your heart and say, "God, is there any unforgiveness in my heart whatsoever?"

I had been a Christian for many years before I saw the significance of forgiveness. The day God wrote those scriptures in neon lights before my eyes was the day I really searched my heart to find out if there was any unforgiveness there, and I discovered there was. A man had stolen $12,000 from our ministry through a dishonest business dealing, and we had some real unforgiveness against him. When we realized this, we forgave him, and within two weeks God sent us a check for $50,000 for the ministry from a totally different source! Forgiveness pays off!

Sometimes we don't activate all of the mind of Christ that is available to us because we don't really understand all of the things God's Word says. Jesus did not go around with unforgiveness in His heart so we should not feel justified when we say, "Well, look at what he did to me. I have a right not to forgive him." God and Jesus want us to forgive anyone whom we have anything against so there will be no hindrance to our prayers.

I almost explode when I think about such a wonderful loving Father who says we can have anything we say, providing we have no doubt that we're going to receive it, and then providing we do not have unforgiveness in our hearts. Because we do have the very mind of Christ, we are going to forgive those who have sinned against us at all times.

"Now it came to pass in those days that He went out to the mountain to pray, and continued all night in prayer to God" (Luke 6:12). Since we have the mind of Christ, what would happen to us if we began to give one night a month (not even one night a week) but just one night a month to do nothing but pray. What would happen to our prayer life. Wow!

Did you ever have insomnia? Instead of looking on that as a problem, look upon it as a blessing, and think how wonderful it would be if we took those waking times to just talk to God!

Jesus had a wonderful prayer life because He

had an open communication line to God at all times. Because we possess the same mind Jesus had, we, too, can have an open communication to the heavenly Father at all times. God is as close as your spiritual telephone; all you have to do is pick it up and you'll never get a busy signal with God.

Here's a great verse to remember: *"So shall My word be that goes forth from my mouth; It shall not return to me void, But it shall accomplish what I please, And it shall prosper in the thing for which I sent it"* (Isaiah 55:11).

If we are going to have the same kind of prayer life Jesus had, we are going to have to stand on God's Word and know there is no promise in the Word of God that is ever going to return to us void. We are going to know we can rely on every promise in the Word of God, because not one word of it has ever failed!

When we pray we need to know the things we can receive. Possessing the mind of Christ will keep us within the Word of God and will give us a desire to pray for the things of God to be completed in our life, rather than the lust and the pleasures in this world.

We're going to have belief and not doubt in our hearts. Sometimes we look at the circumstances and think there is absolutely no way out. And yet I wonder what we might have done under the same circumstances had we been Jesus when He was nailed to the cross. Would we have thought at that particular time, "God has forgotten all about me?" Would we have looked at the circumstances and said, "This is it, I've had it?" Would we have let fear grip us when we went down into the very depths of hell itself, or would we have known that our prayer to God was answered and that God would protect us in all areas?

Jesus prayed, *"O My Father, if it is possible, let this cup pass from Me; nevertheless, not as I will, but as You will"* (Matthew 26:39). He knew the purpose for which He had been sent to earth. He knew when He went into hell He was going to come right out of there and sit at the right hand of God, the Father Almighty. There was no doubt whatsoever in His mind about His resurrection.

Beloved, let us believe as Jesus did. Let us believe in the promises of God without doubt, without unbelief, without compromise, without waivering. Let us possess and use the mind of Christ where prayer is concerned.

What about Treasures?

"Do not lay up for yourselves treasures on earth, where moth and rust destroy and where thieves break in and steal; but lay up for yourselves treasures in heaven, where neither moth nor rust destroys and where thieves do not break in and steal. For where your treasure is, there your heart will be also" (Matthew 6:19-21).

Because one of our most priceless posessions is the mind of Christ, we have the same attitudes and same thoughts as Jesus Christ. We are not going to be interested in storing up things for ourself down here.

I once heard a Catholic priest say, "The only thing a dead man holds in his hands are the things he has given to God." How true. When they put your body in a casket, they can put a fur coat on you, they can wrap you in your finest mink, they can load your hands with diamonds, but it won't do the least bit of good. All we are going to take out of this earth are the things we've given to God. We ought to be extremely interested in our heavenly bank accounts.

One of the best deposits we can ever make into our heavenly bank account is a deposit slip showing the names of the souls of people who might not have ever met Jesus if we had not shared the gospel with them. We can give glory to God, which is one of the greatest ways I know of to store up treasures in heaven. We can lay hands on the sick and heal them and we know this gives God tremendous joy. Put those things in your bank account which add up in heaven instead of earthly bank accounts which mean nothing to God!

Possessing the mind of Christ means that you are not going to be laying up the glory of this world.

You are not going to be laying up the glory of this world.

You are not going to be laying up the deceit of this world.

You are not going to be storing up the kind of riches down here which people think are so important. Sometimes we think this means only money but there are many other things people feel bring glory.

How many times have we seen TV and Hollywood stars rise up rapidly to fame and fortune. All their earthly treasures are invested in the flimsy values and glory which temporarily accompanies them. When their world crashes, they and their earthly treasures often end in suicide.

The Word says, *"Lay up for yourself treasure in heaven."* What are our treasures? They are the very desires of our hearts—the very things we hold near and dear to us.

Let the things that you hold dear be exactly the things Jesus valued. Whad did He value? The souls of men, the health and healing of men, the deliverance of men. He held the power of God dear to His heart. He held God dear to His heart.

If we are to store up treasures in heaven where nothing can ever get in and disturb them or destroy them, we must learn to develop the same attributes Jesus had so we can store the things that are pleasing to God in our heavenly bank account, the things that *are* the very mind of Christ.

Matthew 11:28 gives us some wonderful words from Jesus. *"Come unto Me, all you who labor and are heavy laden, and I will give you rest. Take My yoke upon you and learn from me, for I am gentle and lowly in heart, and you will find rest for your souls. For My yoke is easy and My burden is light."*

I'm going to believe with all my heart, my mind, my body and my soul that the yoke Jesus gives us is not a heavy yoke. His burden is light. We do not have to be burdened down with the cares of the world, we do not have to be worried all the time because He says, "You take my yoke because my burden is light, and I'll take care of your life for you."

I especially love the Amplified version. He says, *"I will ease and relieve and refresh your souls."* (Verse 30) *"My yoke is wholesome, useful (useful, good)—not harsh, hard, sharp or pressing, but comfortable, gracious and pleasant; and My burden is light and easy to be borne."* Glory, give all your burdens to Him!

We know all these wonderful promises of God, but we need to have them brought to the surface occasionally in a different way, or at a different time. An "oldie" that is a favorite of mine is, *"The Kingdom of Heaven is like a treasure a man discovered in a field. In his excitement, he sold everything he owned to get enough money to buy the field—and get the treasure, too! Again, the Kingdom of Heaven is lika a pearl merchant on the lookout for choice pearls. he discovered a real bargain—a pearl of great value—and sold everything he owned to purchase it!"* (Matthew 13:44,45 TLB).

Possessing the mind of Christ, we should see exactly what Jesus was saying. Very simply He was saying, "If you will give up everything and follow me, then that is worth more than anything in the whole world. It's worth everything to follow me!" One man sold *everything* to receive the treasure in the field, and one man sold *everything* to get the pearl of great price.

The pearl of great price in all of our lives is not a pearl we can wear around our neck, not a pearl we can put in a ring on our finger, but a pearl we keep in our heart, that personal relationship with the Lord Jesus Christ. Nothing on this earth can compare with the privilege of having a personal relationship with the Lord Jesus Christ. There are no treasures on this earth; there is no money on this earth; there are no riches on this earth which will compare with the knowledge that we personally have Jesus Christ in our hearts!

We need to "sell" ourselves for the pearl of great price!

Another of my favorite portions of scripture that I try to practice is found in Matthew 6:25-34: *"So my counsel is: "Don't worry about things— food, drink, and clothes. For you already have life and a body—and they are far more important than what to eat and wear. Look at the birds! They don't worry about what to eat—they don't need to sow or reap or store up food—for your heavenly Father feeds them. And you are far more valuable to him than they are. Will all your worries add a single moment to your life? And why worry about your clothes? Look at the field lilies! They don't worry about theirs. Yet King Solomon in all his glory was not clothed as beautifully as they. And if God cares so wonderfully for flowers that are here today and gone tomorrow, won't he more surely care for you, O men of little faith? So don't worry at all about having enough food and clothing. Why be like the heathen? For they take pride in all these things and are deeply concerned about them. But your heavenly Father already knows perfectly well that you need them, and he will give them to you if you give him first place in your life and live as he wants you to. So don't be anxious about tomorrow. God will take care of your tomorrow, too. Live one day at a time"(TLB).*

We worry and worry and worry about how we are going to be fed. What is going to happen during the famine which is coming? What is going to happen to inflation? What is going to happen with recession? Why worry? The Bible specifically tells us not to be like the heathen, who worry, but to be like the field lilies.

Philippians 4:19 says, *"But my God shall supply all your needs according to His riches in glory by Christ Jesus"* (KJV).

He will, without a shadow of a doubt, take care of me and my family as long as we are in His will. I know that I know that I know this to be a fact. God says it, so I believe it! He also says to work hard and to use common sense, so He doesn't agree to do *my* part in my earthly responsibilities. I have to do my part.

Thinking along the lines of Jesus, we know that God will provide for our every need; therefore, I am not going to worry about the things of today. I am not going to worry about the problems which might come up tomorrow because I know that God is going to take care of them.

What do I do instead of worrying? I take Matthew 6:33 and pretend that it is a press-on decal and I iron it right onto my heart. *"But seek ye first the kingdom of God, and His righteousness; and all these things shall be added unto you"* (KJV). The

Living Bible so beautifully and simply expresses it by saying, *"He will give them to you if you give him first place in your life and live as he wants you to."*

The best annuities and insurance you can have in the entire world is simply a decision to give God first place in your life and then you will have that beautiful peace which says that God will take care of every need you have.

Seek first of all the very righteousness of God. Seek to possess the mind of Christ at all times. Seek to use the mind of Christ at all times. Seek to think with the mind of Christ at all times. Then, and only then will you find that all of these things will be added unto you.

One of the greatest examples of that verse in my personal life concerned marriage. When I met Charles, I could not see how I could possibly get married. God had placed such a call upon my life that I knew I had no choice except to serve Him.

Being a housewife just didn't fit into the schedule God had given me. And yet, God had suddenly put a charming man in my path. My heart was beating for Charles. My very soul was crying out for Charles. Because of the call God had put on my life, I could not see any possible way to get married and fit a husband into my life.

One Sunday afternoon, in a spare bedroom of a pastor's home in Florida, God spoke to me very distinctly. "You are to marry Charles," He said. "Because you have sought first my kingdom and my righteousness, I am going to add a husband to your life—a husband to protect you, a husband to take care of you, a husband to love you all of the days of your life."

Had I sought Charles as a husband, I probably would not be Mrs. Charles Hunter today. Because I sought first the kingdom of God and His righteousness, because possessing the mind of Christ kept my mind on the things of God instead of the things that I might naturally want as a woman, God rewarded my obedience. He brought me the desire of my heart—the most wonderful loving husband in the whole world.

We need to develop our mind to the point where we will have such a craving and such a hunger for the Word of God that nothing else will satisfy us. Because nothing else will satisfy us, we will continue to seek, to search, to look for, to pursue and to hunt for nothing but the kingdom of God! And then we will be so blessed to discover how all of these other things will, little by little and one by one, be added unto us.

Possessing the mind of Christ is the most beautiful, simple, easy way in the world to receive all of the desires of your heart.

Matthew 7:21 (KJV) shows us another beautiful way to know whether or not we really do possess the mind of Christ. *"Not every one that saith unto me, Lord, Lord, shall enter into the kingdom of heaven; but he that doeth the will of my Father which is in heaven."*

It is not because we say, "Lord, Lord," that makes the difference.

Possessing the mind of Christ means that we are

going to do the will of God.

We are not going to argue.

We are not going to disagree.

We are not going to have sessions on why we don't want to do what the Word of God says.

We are going to do the will of the Father. And what is His will? His Word is His will. We will simply obey His Word.

CHAPTER THIRTEEN

WHAT DOES JESUS SAY ABOUT "BEING A DOER OF THE WORD"

A lot has been said in recent years concerning being a doer of the Word, and yet, enough could never be said to let us know what Jesus really thinks about it, and how serious He is about us being "doers" of the Word!

Matthew 7:24 puts a real good thought into our mind. Jesus says, *"Therefore whoever hears these sayings of Mine, and DOES them, I will liken him to a wise man who built his house on the rock: and the rain descended, and the floods came, and the winds blew and beat on that house; and it did not fall, for it was founded on the rock. Now, everyone who hears these sayings of Mine, and does not DO them, will be like a foolish man who built his house on the sand: and the rain descended, and the floods came, and the winds blew and beat on that house; and it fell. And great was its fall."*

For many years Charles and I thought when Jesus spoke about the man who built his house on sand, He was talking about the sinner. But, do you

know who that man really is? That is the individual
who hears the Word of God, but does not become a
doer of the Word. He simply sits down and absorbs
the Word of God. Possibly he goes to church every
Sunday morning, Sunday night, and maybe even on
Wednesday. However, he never actually gets out
and does anything for the Lord Jesus Christ. Jesus
said that is not only the sinner, but the one who has
heard the Word of God and doesn't do it. That born-
again, Spirit-filled person is going to be just as bad
off as the man who never really heard the gospel and
never accepted Jesus into his life.

One of the most exciting places where Jesus
talks about becoming a doer of the Word is recorded
in the fourteenth chapter in the book of John, where
He is so emphatic about the doer becoming a "real"
doer. He says in the twelfth verse: *"Most assuredly, I
say to you, he who believes in me, the works that I do
he will DO also; and greater works than these he
will DO, because I go to My Father."*

He healed the sick. He made the lame to walk.
He made the blind to see. He cast out devils. He
raised the dead, and then He turned right around
and said that we were going to DO exactly the same
things. He didn't say we would have the potential or
the ability to DO these things, but that we would actually be out DOING all the things He did.

He walked on the water. He calmed the sea. He
sent demons into pigs. He turned water into wine.
He fed the 5,000 with four loaves and fishes. He
reached out and loved the world that needs to be
loved.

What a special place for us to sit. What a special place we occupy in the heart of God. What a glory we are to God when we believe the things Jesus said, and go on to perform those same things.

Jesus told the woman at the well that she had no husband and the man she was now living with was not her husband. Spirit-filled believers can also operate in this gift. Not only can they, they should, because we have this ability when we possess the mind of Christ.

Jesus says if you are a real believer in Him, you will believe totally and completely that He is the way, the truth and the life, that He is the resurrection and the life, that He is the true vine and His Father is the gardener. You are going to believe that all the things He did should be happening today, and not only are you going to believe that, you are going to be DOING the same things He did.

Then He gives one of the greatest promises in His Word when he says you and I are going to DO even greater works than He did because He was going to His Father.

In the book SUPERNATURAL HORIZONS we wrote about many of the greater things God had quickened in our spirits that the Body of Christ is going to DO. The thing that is so important to realize about this verse is not our capability for doing it, but our availability to DO the greater things that God said we would DO.

That is a totally mind-boggling statement. If we can just get the magnitude of that promise so inside our spirit, if we can grab onto it and hold onto it, if we can nurture it and carry it through to fulfillment, there is absolutely no limit to what God can do through us.

Over and over again as Jesus called His disciples, He called them into a life of action. He did not call them into a life of sitting on a pew. Over and over again as He called them to become disciples, the Bible says, *"Immediately, they left their nets and followed Him."*

Did God ever tell you to do something that you failed to do *immediately*? That is a word which needs to be inserted in our vocabulary where God is concerned. We question whether it's God or the devil, we have to wait until we have had two or three confirmations from someone else, and by this time the opportunity to do something immediately for God has gone by. When God tells us to do something, we should do it right now!

Alan Granger, a young Jewish pastor of The Church of the Crosses in LasCruces, N.M. shared a dream with us that made a tremendous impression on me. There's a great message here.

I dreamed that I was someplace like the Sahara Desert. I likened it to when I was in the Sinai Desert, or Saudi Arabia where there are miles and miles of sand dunes. Then suddenly I saw cities come right straight up out of the sand. These were big sandstone cities, the old Aladdin type, and I was sitting there when a man pulled up in a red Ferrari. I was conscious that there was a city here, and another one down the road, and then another one that I could just see out in the distance. These cities looked almost like ships on the ocean. The Lord was telling me right then that this was a message for the whole world, and not for one area.

The man pulled up in the red Ferrari. I saw him as a man who gives to God and a man who loves God. As he pulled up in the car, he got out and I saw he was very proud of what he was doing. You could tell he was real excited. He said, "This is MY red Ferrari, and it's worth $58,000."

I said, "That's great, it's a beautiful car."

He said, "Do you know what I've been thinking about? God told me to give you this car and I've been thinking about all those plans you've got." Then he mentioned three projects I had been wanting to do and had actually been planning for, but was unable to start on them because of a lack of finances.

He continued, "God told me to give you this car and if I gave it to you and you sold it, you could get $58,000 for it. Then you could put so much toward the first project, so much toward the second project, and the balance on the third project and you would have all three of them going. Then you could go on and do the bigger thing you've been wanting to do."

I said, "That's possible. What are you going to do?

He said, "I don't know. I'm THINKING about it."

At that moment I became so angry I was shaking because I was scared and mad. The combination of being both scared and angry made me almost terrified of this man. As terrified as you would be if you walked into a room not believing in divine healing and someone told you that they had AIDS after you had just finished shaking their hand. I had that kind of mortal fear plus I was angry beyond anything I had ever been in my entire life.

I started backing up from him and rebuking him. I pointed my finger at him and said, "You are cursed along with the car!"

He was shocked! He said, "Why?"

I replied, "Because you're THINKING about doing God's will when you already KNOW God's will; when it's been explained to you and you SEE the logic of it and you SEE the NEED of it and you're "THINKING" about doing God's will." Irate, I continued, "How dare you hold God in bondage?"

Just then the big city wall behind him began to crumble. The noise made him look up and it was very obvious a big rock was going to come crashing down on the car and him. He looked up and yelled, "Take the car, take the keys, take the car!"

Sadly, I explained, "You're trying to give me the car to save your own skin right now. You and the car will perish together."

At that moment the rock came down and I saw his blood fly everywhere. The car was totally demolished because the rock was larger than both the car and the man.

As I turned around, the people had come out of every city as far as the eye could see. I mean millions and millions and tens of millions of people. The ones in front were all looking at me with the same look on their face, asking the same unspoken question. A couple of people in the front said, "Well, what about us?"

I said, "You could have given to God when He asked you to and it would have saved your soul, but now you'll lose your soul with it. You and what you wouldn't give to God are going to perish with you."

At that moment all those cities crumbled and a cloud of dust went up. Every person I saw was totally annihilated. There were earthquakes, famine, plagues, and fire falling out of the sky. Sand would instantly burst into flames and consume people as they went screaming off into the night.

This lasted all night long. It was early morning when this man had pulled up in his car. By evening time I was sitting there alone watching while some of the last fires were just starting to burn. It took all day into the night. By morning there was nothing left but smoke and there was not a sound to be heard except the wind whistling through those rocks.

How many times have we said, "I'll have to pray about it," or "I'll have to think about it" when we have heard God and are just stalling for time? Who are you going to pray to when God has told you to do something and you have to "pray about it"? If we really mean business with God, and WANT to do what pleases Him, we should jump at the opportunity to do something when He asks us, but DO IT NOW!

Christianity is a life of action. It is not a passive inactive life. As a matter of fact, it is the most active life I know.

We get excited about doing the "greater things" Jesus said we would do, but we'll never do the greater things until we have done the same things He did.

When Jesus said you were going to become a DOER of the Word, what did He really mean? If you will look at the Great Commission in the sixteenth chapter of Mark, you'll see that He gave us a tremendous number of things to DO. Not to talk about, but to DO!

He said, *"Go into all the world and preach the Gospel to every creature."*

So many times we fail to DO this just because we think, "God, we can't go to Africa," or "We can't go to China or someplace like that." There is a lot of Gospel to be preached on the street on which you live. There's a lot of Gospel to be preached in every supermarket, every store, every restaurant, every airport, every place into which we go.

Jesus said we would have signs and wonders following us. He did not say the signs and wonders were going to be for special believers. He simply said signs and wonders would "follow" every single believer.

A believer has to believe signs and wonders are going to follow him, or they will never follow him. When you come right down to it, if you don't believe in signs and wonders then you're not a believer.

He said we would cast out demons. That's a work, an action that needs to be done. It's not just sitting down in your rocking chair meditating at home, praying and interceding and saying, "Oh, God, I wish you would get those demons out." No, Jesus told us we would be the ones who would cast out demons. Everything He told us to do requires an action.

Then He said, *"They will speak with new tongues."* That's the baptism with the Holy Spirit. He said ALL believers would speak in tongues. He didn't say they were just going to have the opportunity and the ability to do so, He said they would DO IT. Again, another action. If you really want to see real power come into your life, begin to pray more in tongues than you ever have before.

Speaking in tongues should be as natural in your household as speaking in English. We pray far more in tongues than we do in English, because when you pray in tongues you are always praying in the perfect will of God. That's one way to know that you're not praying *outside* the will of God.

We see people running to receive the baptism with the Holy Spirit by the hundreds in our meetings. Praise God they're hungry for the power of God in their lives! If we would all begin to pray at least one hour a day in tongues, our Christian life would develop to new levels!

We need to teach our children to pray in tongues. Parents have a responsibility to see that their children receive the baptism. In the world in which we live today, they need the baptism with the Holy Spirit more than ever before. Let them see you praying in tongues often, and they will do the same thing.

Then, He said we are ALL going to *"lay hands on the sick and they will recover."* Again an action statement, a statement that says, "Get up and go!" A statement that doesn't say, "Stay home and pray for Mary Jones." But get out there and lay your hands on her and believe the Word of God is true so she will be healed.

Charles and I have really learned so much over the years about casting out devils and healing the sick as we have laid hands on hundreds of thousands of people. We have learned that the more we DO, the more we BELIEVE, and the more we see come to pass in our ministry. The number of people who get healed in our miracle crusades today is so far above and beyond what it was just a few years ago that it is almost unbelievable. It is because we have learned to believe more and DO more. When you begin to believe more, then you will DO more. When you DO more, then you begin to believe more. It all works together in a big circle.

Jesus wants us to be a DOER at all times. He wants us to minister to those who need ministering to any place, anywhere, and at any time. Almost every person we see in our daily activity is an opportunity to be a doer of the Word!

One of the greatest things the Body of Christ will ever learn about being a doer of the Word is to look upward and outward instead of inward. We will progress much faster and further in the kingdom of God when we think of others instead of ourselves. So many times we get so involved with our own personal little problems that we are unable to see beyond ourself and our own little nest, lined with one problem after another.

Charles and I have often noticed this principle applies to physical things which might come against us. In my own life when I was so violently attacked with diabetes, I continued to go on and do God's work above and beyond what I physically felt like doing. As a result, God supernaturally and miraculously healed me and returned my dynamic health the devil had tried to take away.

Look up and look out and see what God is doing and how He wants to use you in every area of your life. Then you will be able to see your own problems by the wayside.

CHAPTER 14

WHAT DOES JESUS SAY ABOUT "RESPONSIBILITY OF BELIEVERS IN THE GREAT COMMISSION "

Jesus really poured out His compassionate heart when He spelled out the Great Commission. He gave some real specifics, simply presented so that the world could understand what He was saying, and yet we have ignored His last instructions to us.

None of us have any problem understanding what He said about preaching the gospel, except we pay very little attention to it. *"And He said to them, 'Go into all the world and preach the gospel to every creature. He who believes and is baptized will be saved; but he who does not believe will be condemned.'"* (Mark 16:15,16). Not a single believer could ever misconstrue what Jesus said, and we only have two choices, obey Him or disobey Him. We have grown so fat spiritually the last few years that we have ignored His heart cry to go out and talk to every person we meet so they can know Him as their Savior. We like to send missionaries overseas, but we need to let the heart of Jesus be so in us that our own heart cries with compassion for the lost.

"And these signs will follow those who believe: In My name they will cast out demons; they will speak with new tongues; they will take up serpents; and if they drink anything deadly, it will by no means hurt them; they will lay hands on the sick, and they will recover" (Mark 16:17,18).

In this instance Jesus' heart is not crying out to the sinner, but to the believers—not only to the pastors and evangelists, but to the ordinary, every-day believer. He is telling us that signs and wonders will follow us in our daily walk. He is telling us that we will cast out demons. He is telling us that we will lay hands on the sick and they will recover! If the Bible is true, then let's get on with it and begin to believe that we can do it, too! Not because we make a decision that we can, but because Jesus said it. The only decision we need to make is that we WILL do it.

When you sincerely get the message that the Great Commission is for *all* believers, and not just a few selected "pets" of God who have special abilities, it will change your entire life. That portion of scripture is for each and every one of us, because God doesn't have any "pets".

God has been stressing in our hearts that most of the Body of Christ need to begin to obey the command of Jesus in the Great Commission.

He told all of us to go out into the byways to tell others about Jesus and give them the good news in such a way that they will know Him as their Savior and Lord. Some have learned to minister healing to a few, but EVERY BELIEVER needs to daily lead people to Jesus with signs and wonders following. Jesus used signs, wonders and miracles to convince people that He was the Son of God, the way, the truth, and the light, and we must do exactly that in order to totally fulfill the Great Commission.

Let's begin to obey Him fully! We know of one church in the United States where the members all go into homes nightly, healing the sick, casting out demons, teaching the Word, telling the good news, and leading people into salvation and the baptism with the Holy Spirit. That church has grown from 200 to over 5,000 in about two and a half years. That's fulfilling the Great Commission as Jesus intended for us to do.

What will happen when WE, THE BODY OF CHRIST, receive the heart and compassion of Jesus to win the lost before it is too late? WOW! It's exciting to even think of the potential!

Let us give a testimony of what has happened through the book, TO HEAL THE SICK in just one man's life. THIS CAN HAPPEN TO AND THROUGH YOU, TOO!

Dr. Harvey Lifsey is a teacher-minister who had, along with his associates and team, for years been teaching laymen of foreign countries how to be pastors.

Dr. Lifsey had never really believed in healing, but through a flier he received in the mail, ordered our "Supernatural Special" which included TO HEAL THE SICK, SUPERNATURAL HORIZONS, and ANGELS ON ASSIGNMENT. He thought, "I wonder if there is anything to this supernatural thing."

He was leaving the next day for Ghana and took the healing book with him to read on the plane. He had prepared for three months for his teaching while in Ghana with two associates.

When he arrived in Ghana, he could not leave for two days because of shortage of fuel for the jeep, so the three men were stuck in the hotel for two full days and nights.

He was so excited about what he had read in TO HEAL THE SICK that for the two days the three men took two-hour turns reading the book aloud, absolutely astonished and astounded at what they were learning. They tested it with the Bible and it was all in line with the Word. It reached their spirits, and God said, "Throw away your other teachings and teach these people how to heal the sick."

They taught the first day, and that night over 250 people out of 500 pastors were healed. It actually worked for them and a phenomenal ministry followed.

Dr. Lifsey recently returned from Argentina. Read what he reported with your heart set on how you can add multitudes to the kingdom of God before the return of Jesus. We pray that this will so challenge each reader that you will "Go into all of your world and preach the Gospel, heal the sick, cast out devils, teach the Word, and minister the baptism—as a lay person or a minister!"

Here is Dr. Lifsey's recent testimony sent to us

on a cassette tape:

"Thank you for the 10 cases(800 books) of TO HEAL THE SICK books you gave us to take to Africa. We know those men will be blessed because of the teaching in these fine books. Now let me give you a brief report from our ministry in Argentina.

God is moving there in a mighty way and the people are hungry for God and there is a move of the Spirit among them.

One lay couple, Omar and Marfa, have started preaching in different cities each night, and have taught about 70 other lay people to do the same. This means that thousands are hearing about Jesus every night. Their crowds run from 500 up to as high as 40,000 in a night. These people believe what you teach from the Word of God, and they immediately put it into practice.

The purpose in my being there was to teach about 1,000 lay leaders. The first conference had about 250 and it was the smallest conference we had. One woman who heard the teachings prayed to God, asking how she could put these marvelous truths of the supernatural power of God, the authority and power in Jesus that we taught her, into practice, into operation right now!

She went to the school to pick up her child and saw another mother there who was weeping, so she went to her and asked what was wrong. The woman said her brother was dying of lung cancer. She said, "Oh, I'm a Christian and have learned that we have power and authority in Jesus to heal the sick. May I go to your brother and pray for him?

She went to the home, prayed for the brother, and he was instantly healed. His nephew was his doctor, and the next day the nephew x-rayed his lungs and found him totally healed, and the doctor fell to his knees and said, "This is a miracle of God," and he and his whole family were saved.

Another member of the family was a leader of a major discoteque, a dancing hall. He began to share what God had done and of his finding Christ, and the result was this influential businessman has turned the city upside down! There is a tremendous stir among the people.

I went to preach on my last Sunday night in Rosario, Argentina. This woman about whom I shared above, was a member of this church and was present, along with another woman she had led to the Lord, and another woman the other woman had led to the Lord, and all the family who had been saved as a result of this one woman getting the message that she could heal the sick.

Another man and his wife were burdened about a city about thirty miles away which had no protestant church, so they prayed and went to that city. While walking down the street they saw a woman they had known years before and began talking with her. They went to her home where her husband was dying with cancer of the liver, and the woman had breast cancer. They prayed for them and both of them were instantly healed. They both came to Christ with their families and they immediately started a church in that city and now pastor this house church!

These are just two examples of what is happening with laymen. They are believing God and going out and putting into practice the things that are being taught. I've never seen such hunger for the Word of God anywhere, and the healings that took place are amazing! Everything you can imagine.

One young boy came to a meeting where we were ministering to about 6,000 people. He had been with a group of young people, and was returning from the party, drunk and on drugs when he fell off the train and cracked his head wide open and as a result was paralyzed. His whole body was paralyzed. (His parents brought him to the meeting completely paralyzed.) His head had been shaved and his hair was about ⅛ inch long but you could see the scar about twelve inches long on the side of his head.

During prayer, he was instantly healed, jumped up on a four-foot platform and began running around giving testimony of what God had done for him and was saved.

One woman brought a child who had a tube running down his throat. The child had been diagnosed to have spinal meningitis. Part of the brain was paralyzed and the child was not able to use the throat muscles, could not eat, could not drink, could not suck. It was kept alive with the tube. When we prayed, nothing seemed to happen.

The next night when we again had about 6,000 present, the woman came and gave testimony and showed the child no longer with a tube down its throat, completely healed.

Hundreds, and hundreds, and hundreds were healed. In one service alone we had 6,000 people stand and pray to receive Christ as Savior. God is moving in that nation in a mighty way.

The things we have learned from you and your books have been such a blessing. It has given us a whole new release and we thank God and praise God for you. If these few things can be useful, then let God's kingdom be magnified and His name be glorified. We love you deeply."

How we praise God for what can happen when only one person gets the message that signs and wonders will follow those who believe, and the message that each one of us is to do the works of Jesus.

God is so strongly impressing us to urgently preach to everyone we can that each member of the body of Christ must actually be exactly like Jesus, and DO all the things He did while He was the only Body of Christ on earth.

We challenge every pastor to teach every one in his church how to heal the sick and how to minister salvation and healing, and then send them out two by two into the homes of their city and reach every one in that city for Jesus. It can only be done with signs and wonders following, but when each one believes the simple teachings of Jesus, it will work for you and your people just as it has worked in Argentina and Ghana, as well as in the church that grew to 5,000!

We challenge all believers to discover the way to easily tell people how to know Jesus and to heal the sick so they will do what that one woman did to change her whole city for Jesus.

This is the last of this generation before the return of Jesus, and we MUST WIN THE LOST TO JESUS QUICKLY! Time is rapidly running out and the only ones Jesus has to do His work are those of us who believe.

God has prepared the hearts of the sinners so much that we hardly need to mention the name of Jesus and they are ready to accept Him. They have tried everything else, including religion, and found that nothing has given them the peace for which they are searching. God is trying to get His children prepared to go tell the sinners what a great thing He has in store for those who will believe in Jesus. We are the only ones He has to do this job and if we don't do it, people will go into hell forever.

We believe God will baptize you with fire as well as the Holy Spirit, and put a zeal and boldness into you to do mighty works for Him, just like those in Ghana and Argentina are doing. That is His calling for each of us. Charles and I cannot stop because we have such a burning in our very souls for the lost.

At the meeting where the blue flame appeared, God told us to tell the people if they would not go out and do His work as Jesus had commanded that He would walk over the heads of the Spirit-filled Christians and save the drug addicts and the outcast and put His Spirit in them and a zeal and compassion in them, and send them out to do His work because He was going to get His work accomplished.

Charles just made and interesting statement to

me as I was finishing the "Glory" chapter. He said, "Honey, the glory of God that I really want to see is the hundreds, the thousands, maybe even the millions of people we have touched through our crusades, through television and through our books begin to do exactly the same things we are doing—operate in the glory of God; go out and lay hands on the sick and bring people into the kingdom of God."

When you come right down to it, what is the greatest thing in the world you could see? Hundreds of thousands of people coming to Jesus as a result of something *you* did.

When we possess the mind of Christ we want to fulfill the wishes of God; we want to do everything God wants us to do; we want to see the world saved; we want to see the world reclaimed, we want to see the world led into the kingdom of God. It's not God's wish that any should perish. It's not the wish of Jesus that any should perish. It is their wish that ALL should be saved!

Say with Isaiah and with us, "HERE AM I, LORD, SEND ME!"